r

CREATING THE CONDITIONS FOR CLASSROOM IMPROVEMENT

A Handbook of Staff Development Activities

David Hopkins

Mel West

Mel Ainscow

Alma Harris

John Beresford

David Fulton Publishers
London

David Fulton Publishers Ltd
2 Park Square, Milton Park, Abingdon, Oxon, OX14 4RN

www.fultonpublishers.co.uk

First published in Great Britain by David Fulton Publishers 1997
Reprinted 1999, 2000, 2001

Transferred to Digital Printing 2007

Note: The rights of David Hopkins, Mel West, Mel Ainscow, Alma Harris and
John Beresford to be identified as the authors of this work has been asserted by
them in accordance with the Copyright, Designs and Patents Act 1988.

Copyright © David Hopkins, Mel West, Mel Ainscow, Alma Harris and John
Beresford 1997

British Library Cataloguing in Publication Data.
A catalogue record for this book is available from the British Library

ISBN 1–85346–474–0

Typeset by Sheila Knight, London

Publisher's Note
The publisher has gone to great lengths to ensure the quality of this reprint
but points out that some imperfections in the original may be apparent

Contents

Acknowledgements

Over the past seven years we have been privileged to work closely with the sixty or so schools participating in the 'Improving the Quality of Education for All' (IQEA) school improvement project. Although our purpose has been to assist them in managing the process of change, we have learned far more from them than we could ever have contributed to their progress. Whatever virtue our work has, it is only the result of the insight, commitment, tolerance and good humour of our friends in the IQEA network. Thank you.

We are also grateful to our colleagues at the University of Nottingham, the University of Cambridge School of Education and the University of Manchester for their continuing support of the IQEA Project. In particular we are grateful to Carol Mee and Avril Rathbone for the secretarial help provided during the preparation of this book. We acknowledge too David Fulton and John Owens of David Fulton Publishers, who despite our cavalier attitude towards publishers' deadlines, believe sufficiently in our work that they continue to share it with a wider audience.

In preparing this school improvement handbook, we have inevitably drawn on our other published work which we acknowledge here and in the reference list. In particular: more detailed descriptions of the IQEA process are found in *School Improvement in an Era of Change* (Hopkins *et al.* 1994) and *Improving the Quality of Education for All* (Hopkins *et al.* 1996); and a more theoretical treatment of the 'classroom conditions' is found in the journal *Teachers and Teaching: Theory and Practice* (Hopkins *et al.* 1998). This book follows closely the pattern established by its companion volume *Creating the Conditions for School Improvement* (Ainscow *et al.* 1994).

CHAPTER 1

Improving the Quality of Education for All

Introduction

During the past seven years or so we have been working closely with schools in East Anglia, North London, Yorkshire, Humberside, the East Midlands, as well as Iceland, Puerto Rico and South Africa on a school improvement and development project known as *Improving the Quality of Education for All* (IQEA). The overall aim of the project is to strengthen the schools' ability to provide quality education for all its pupils by building upon existing good practice. In so doing, we are also producing and evaluating a model of school development, and using the opportunity of collaboration with schools in the IQEA network to conduct a long-term investigation into the processes of school change and student achievement.

As we work with schools within the framework of a national reform agenda we are committed to an approach to educational change that focuses on student achievement *and* the school's ability to cope with change. We refer to this particular approach as *school improvement*. We regard school improvement as a distinct approach to educational change that enhances student outcomes *as well as* strengthening the school's capacity for managing improvement initiatives. In this sense school improvement is about raising student achievement through focusing on the *teaching/learning* process and those conditions which support it.

The IQEA school improvement project works from an assumption that schools are most likely to strengthen their ability to provide enhanced outcomes for all pupils when they adopt ways of working that are consistent with both their own aspirations as a school community and the current reform agenda. Indeed, the schools we are working with are using the impetus of external reform for internal purposes as they navigate the systemic changes of recent years.

At the outset of IQEA we attempted to outline our own vision of school improvement by articulating a set of principles that provided us with a philosophical and practical starting point. These principles were offered to schools as the basis for collaboration in the IQEA Project. In short, we were inviting the schools to identify and to work on their own projects and priorities, but to do so in a way which embodied a set of 'core' values about school improvement. These principles represent the expectations we have of the way project schools pursue school improvement. They serve as an *aide-mémoire* to the schools and to ourselves.

The five principles of IQEA are:

- School improvement is a process that focuses on enhancing the quality of students' learning.
- The vision of the school should be one which embraces *all* members of the school community as both learners and contributors.
- The school will see in external pressures for change important opportunities to secure its internal priorities.
- The school will seek to develop structures and create conditions which encourage collaboration and lead to the empowerment of individuals and groups.
- The school will seek to promote the view that enquiry and the monitoring and evaluation quality is a responsibility which all members of staff share.

Although we feel that the operation of these principles can create synergy around change (i.e. together they are greater than the sum of their parts), they characterise an overall approach rather than prescribe a course of action. The intention is that they should inform the thinking and actions of teachers during school improvement efforts and provide a touchstone for the strategies they devise and the behaviours they adopt.

The principles emphasise what we know from experience, as well as from the research on student achievement and school effectiveness, that the greatest impact on student progress is achieved by those innovations or adaptations of practice that intervene in, or modify, the learning process. Changes in curriculum, teaching methods, grouping practices and assessment procedures have the greatest potential impact on the performance of students, and so provide a key focus for school improvement efforts.

Unfortunately the implementation of those changes that positively affect the learning of students is very difficult to achieve. This is because, as Michael Fullan (1991) has pointed out, educational changes that directly impact on the learning of students usually involve teachers in not only adopting new or additional teaching materials, but also in:

- acquiring new *knowledge*
- adopting new *behaviours* (e.g. new teaching styles)
- and, sometimes in modifying their *beliefs or values*.

The implementation 'dip'

It is exactly because change is a process whereby individuals need to 'alter their ways of thinking and doing' that most changes fail to progress beyond early implementation. It is this phenomenon that Fullan (1991) has graphically referred to as 'the implementation dip'. This incorporates that constellation of factors which creates the sense of anxiety and those feelings of incompetence so often associated with relearning and meaningful change. This is the phase of dissonance, of 'internal turbulence', that is as predictable as it is uncomfortable. Many research studies have found that without a period of destabilisation, successful, long-lasting change is unlikely to occur. The implications for school improvement is that conditions need to be created within the school that ensure that individuals are supported through this inevitable but difficult and challenging process.

Conditions for classroom improvement

This is why we have found that within the IQEA Project, *school improvement works best when a clear and practical focus for development is linked to simultaneous work on the internal conditions within the school.* Conditions are the internal features of the school, the 'arrangements' that enable it to get work done. Without an equal focus on conditions, even development priorities that directly affect classroom practice quickly become marginalised. Examples of the conditions that support school improvement are: collaborative planning, staff development, enquiry and reflection, and the involvement of students. Experience of the IQEA Project suggests that work on these conditions results in the creation of opportunities for teachers to feel more powerful and confident about change.

The IQEA approach to school improvement is based on our experience that effective change strategies focus not only on the implementation of school-selected policies, or chosen initiatives, but also on creating the conditions within schools that can sustain the teaching/learning process. A previous book in this series, *Creating the Conditions for School Improvement,* focused primarily upon creating the school-level conditions for improvement (Ainscow *et al.* 1994).

As our work has progressed, we have found it necessary to establish certain conditions within the classroom alongside those at the level of the school. We have recently been elaborating such a set of classroom conditions designed to assist teachers in facilitating the learning of all students. In this book we present our initial conceptualisation of those classroom conditions which we have found necessary for sustainable school improvement.

Who is the book for?

In writing this book we have had in mind the teacher, or indeed groups of teachers, interested in classroom-level change and development. In some cases such individuals may have assumed responsibility for development work in the school. It may be a head, or deputy, the appraisal or curriculum coordinator, the person in charge of staff development, or of drawing up the school's development plan. It may even be a head of department or faculty who has a clear view of effective teaching and wishes to extend this view by working with colleagues. In short, this book is for anyone in a school who is taking responsibility for some form of development activity.

What does the book do?

This book is not about what changes should be introduced into a school but instead it focuses upon creating the conditions for *supporting* those changes which lead to improvement in the classroom and the school. To be effective at managing change, schools and teachers need to modify the internal conditions of the classroom *at the same time* as introducing changes in teaching or the curriculum. The book therefore provides ideas and materials to help colleagues in school to create such conditions in classrooms and offers a strategic approach to staff development.

How should the book be used?

This book is not a step-by-step guide to classroom improvement. In our experience such 'quick-fix' approaches, although superficially attractive, rarely work in practice. Although schools can use similar broad approaches and strategies to develop, there is no one way that is right for every school. Consequently, the book provides different starting points and strategies for teachers in varying contexts and situations. These staff development resources are intended to be used within the context of the school's own aspirations. A key task of those using the suggestions and materials provided here will be to decide which of them are most suitable and for what purpose.

How is the book organised?

As part of our work with schools we have identified six key conditions necessary for effective classroom development. The bulk of the book is taken up with describing in individual chapters what these conditions are, and in presenting staff development exercises on how they can be encouraged. Prior to this in-depth look at the classroom conditions, we present a brief account of our current school improvement work and a rationale for the 'conditions' approach. At the end of the book we make some suggestions as to how a school can develop its own school and classroom improvement strategy.

Some people may find it helpful to read the book cover to cover as an introduction to classroom improvement. Others, having a clear idea of where they are going, may wish just to plunder it for staff development activities. Both are fine by us – we hope that the book is organised sufficiently clearly to allow for both approaches, as well as those in between.

Where do the ideas come from?

This book is based on our school improvement work which we have been pursuing in various guises and in different combinations of collaboration since the late 1980s. Although we are, for some of our life, university teachers, we also work intensively with schools as facilitators of the change process; there are now almost a hundred schools in our network. As a consequence the book is grounded in practice, but also tested by reference to the available research evidence. Those who are interested in pursuing these ideas further should consult our other texts on this subject, e.g. *School Improvement in an Era of Change* (Hopkins *et al.* 1994) and *Improving the Quality of Education for All* (Hopkins *et al.* 1996), which both give a more theoretical perspective, but also provide many practitioner accounts of school-based work on the improvement conditions.

It is appropriate therefore that this second practical handbook is about 'creating the conditions for classroom improvement'. Despite the abundance of policy initiatives and change efforts, too little of it positively affects classroom practice. We hope that this book will help in some way to get those useful and helpful changes behind the classroom door.

CHAPTER 2

Creating the conditions for classroom improvement

Introduction

We have already noted that one of the early findings from the IQEA Project was that *school improvement works best when a clear and practical focus for development is linked simultaneously to work on the internal conditions of the school.* This led us to develop and test a strategy for school improvement based on such a twin focus. As we have also noted, the conditions identified during the early phases of the project were related to school-level conditions, or the school's management arrangements, although of course many of the schools' priorities were classroom-based (Hopkins *et al.* 1994). But, in line with contemporary school effects research, we too were finding that it is necessary to modify the conditions within the classroom, as well as those at the level of the school, if school improvement strategies are to fully impact on student achievement (Creemers 1994, Joyce and Showers 1995, Joyce *et al.* 1997). We have therefore been elaborating a set of class-room conditions that enable teachers to facilitate the learning of all students. In this chapter we outline our 'conditions' approach to school improvement and then present an initial conceptualisation of the classroom conditions necessary for a sustainable school improvement strategy.

Rationale

The research on both school and teacher effects draws on similar epistemological models to generate knowledge. Put simply, they follow a process-product research design. High levels of student achievement are identified and 'backward mapped' to identify those school and teacher characteristics that correlate with high levels of student outcome. This research effort has over the past twenty years yielded impressive results and given us rich and detailed descriptions of the characteristics of effective schools and classrooms.

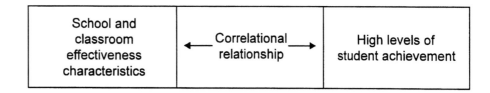

School and classroom effectiveness characteristics	Correlational relationship	High levels of student achievement

For those of us committed to improving as well as understanding the effectiveness of schools and classrooms, the research on school and class-room effects has one major weakness. Because the relationship between these characteristics and student outcomes is one of association, it tells us little about how one affects the other.

Conditions

It is the hiatus between the school/teacher characteristics on the one hand, and enhanced levels of student achievement on the other, that provides the focus for our work. We work from an assumption that there are a set of intervening variables operating at the school and classroom level that mediate between the characteristics of effectiveness on the one hand and enhanced levels of student achievement on the other. It is this emphasis on the *enabling conditions* at both the classroom and school levels that distinguishes our work from colleagues who operate within the school effectiveness tradition, and indeed from many of those who intervene in schools and classrooms for the purposes of improvement.

It is the enabling conditions that allow the 'process' to affect the 'product'. A simple example illustrates the point. It is now well established that co-operative group instruction has a positive impact on student achievement (e.g. Slavin 1993, Joyce *et al.* 1987, Johnson and Johnson 1989). Knowing that, however, is not enough. We also need to know what conditions have to be in place inside the school to allow the teaching approach to impact upon student achievement. These conditions will obviously vary from school to school, but it is fair to suggest that the full impact of this teaching strategy will not be achieved without a degree of school- and classroom-based *staff development*, some *enquiry and reflection* on progress made, and the *involvement of students* in the teaching and learning process. In order for this teaching strategy to have a whole-school impact there would also be a need for *leadership* at all levels in order to initiate and sustain the momentum, some *collaborative planning* to ensure direction, and *coordination* of the activity throughout the school. Our previous work has enabled us to produce a formulation at the school level that gives us some confidence to proceed (Hopkins *et al.* 1994).

Innovations in teaching and learning designed to enhance student achievement, e.g. cooperative group work	Enabling conditions ← or capacity building → in the school	High levels of student achievement

Although this focus on 'enabling conditions' or 'enhancing the school's capacity' for innovation and change draws on the implementation research (see, for example, Fullan 1991), it is an idea that is still not well understood. Although the words that we use to describe the enabling conditions contain similarities to those found on the lists of school effectiveness characteristics, there are qualitative differences between them. The 'gap' between characteristics and outcome that we encounter frequently in our ongoing research and development work with schools requires a much more radical and sophisticated understanding of school change than just simply translating the school-level characteristics into 'doing words'. To take our (Hopkins *et al.* 1994:3) definition of school improvement as 'a distinct approach to educational change that enhances student achievement as well as strengthening the school's capacity for managing change seriously' requires a fundamental rethinking of strategies for innovation and change based on a transcendence and reintegration of our current frameworks of knowledge and action (West and Hopkins 1996, Hopkins 1996).

Capacity   Besides the focus on capacity building, while at the same time working on strategies that enhance student achievement, there is another characteristic to the enabling conditions that is worth mentioning here. If the concern is to help teachers modify their behaviour in order to enhance the learning of their students then it is necessary to use the language and frames of reference that reflects the experience of teachers. Although this may appear an obvious point, Sally Brown and her colleagues (1995:6) argue on the basis of their recent research that:

> the ways in which teachers conceptualise pupils' progress, and the kind of classroom support that is required to promote that progress, are much more complex and rich than the conceptions of progress and support implicit [in the] school effectiveness research.

The disjuncture between the language of research and the language of teachers is, in our experience, a major barrier to innovation and development in schools. Unless a school improvement strategy reflects the implicit theories of practitioners, then it will in our experience be doomed to failure. This is not to argue however that the teacher's view is necessarily correct, or complete; if it were then there would be little need for school improvement. But it is to argue that change efforts need to begin with the experience of teachers and to work at the level of the classroom to sustain change at the level of the organisation.

Michael Fullan (1995) makes a similar point in his recent critique of 'The school as a learning organisation':

> If schools as learning organisations are not to be a distant dream, he argues, teachers need to expand their notions of teaching within the context of capacity building and action enquiry. Changes in teaching practice only occur when there is clarity and coherence in the minds of teachers.

In terms of the traditional language of change, for strategies that are concerned with student achievement, this clarity needs to be at the receiving end rather than at the delivery end. In other words, researchers and policy-makers may have very clear strategies for change and improvement, but unless these connect with the understanding of realities of teachers this increasing clarity at the top will only increase incoherence at the bottom.

It is ideas such as these that have informed our approach to school improvement. The need to build capacity whilst enhancing the teaching/learning process, and the importance of working from the language, theories and experience of teachers are very much part of our ways of working. This is the rationale for our research into developing the classroom conditions for school improvement.

7

Original conceptualisation

Our framework for school improvement is based on our experience that effective change strategies focus not only on the implementation of centralised policies or chosen initiatives, but also on creating the conditions within schools that can sustain the teaching/learning process. Unless this is done, the impact of any development will only be tangential to the central purpose of educational change – the enhanced achievement of students. As we have already indicated, from our work on the IQEA Project, we have identified a series of school-level conditions that underpin the work of these successful schools (Hopkins *et al.* 1994). Broadly stated these conditions are:

- staff development
- involvement
- leadership
- coordination
- enquiry and reflection
- collaborative planning.

Overview of the 'classroom conditions' research

These six conditions were the focus of our early work with the IQEA Project schools. More recently, we have begun to focus some of our research energies onto what we originally thought were a parallel set of conditions which relate to the notion of capacity at the classroom level. These conditions were connected in our minds to teacher development, much in the same way as the original set of conditions were to school development. As such they were supposed to be transferable across classrooms and between teachers and related to a variety of teaching/learning initiatives designed to enhance the achievement of students. At this stage in the work we adapted and simplified our original framework (as illustrated in Hopkins *et al.* 1994) to express the relationship, as we then saw it, between school and classroom conditions, and the process of change in schools. This relationship is seen in Figure 2.1.

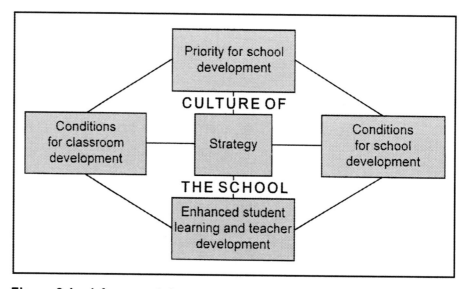

Figure 2.1 A framework for school improvement

During the academic year 1994–95, we began a systematic observation and enquiry programme that focused on the *classroom conditions for school improvement*. Besides drawing on the experience of all the schools in the IQEA network, we identified a number of 'research schools' whose own development priorities were strongly committed to teaching and learning, and who were prepared to collaborate with us on our research agenda.

We constructed an initial agenda of research questions that were shared with the collaborating schools and that complemented their own particular interests in the area of teaching and learning. Our initial questions were framed upon about three overlapping areas related to the development of classroom practice. These are:

- *conceptual issues*, i.e. what are the classroom conditions that can help facilitate the learning of all pupils?
- *methodological issues*, i.e. how can teachers within a school establish the extent to which these conditions are in place?
- *strategic issues*, i.e. how can teachers be helped to improve these conditions?

The tasks implied by these questions are set out in Table 2.1.

Table 2.1 Classroom conditions that help to facilitate the learning of all students: research agenda and tasks

Research focus	Research questions	Tasks
Conceptualising classroom conditions	What are the classroom conditions that can help facilitate the learning of all pupils?	Literature review and school-based observation and enquiry
Auditing classroom conditions	How can teachers within a school establish the extent to which these conditions are in place?	Developing techniques for mapping classroom conditions
Developing classroom conditions	How can teachers be helped to improve these conditions?	Staff development activities to support the enhancement and spread of classroom conditions

The *conceptual* issue is being addressed through academic papers and the background documentation that supports it (e.g. Beresford 1995a). The *methodological* focus has resulted in the questionnaire scale, contained in the Appendix, that measures teachers' perceptions of the quality of the classroom conditions existing in the school (Beresford 1995b). The scale is modelled on the 'conditions of school' questionnaire already extensively used within the IQEA Project and more generally by researchers interested in mapping the process of change (Cambridge University 1994, Ainscow *et al.* 1995). The *strategic* concern is being met by the production of this handbook as a companion edition to that already published on the school-level conditions (Ainscow *et al.* 1994).

The nature of this collaborative enquiry involved a series of partnerships between the research schools and the research team. The work progressed through a series of three phases.

Phase 1

An initial analysis of the classroom conditions was developed based on our ongoing experience on the IQEA Project and initial reviews of the literature.

Phase 2

The initial analysis of the classroom conditions was subject to critical scrutiny at a series of day conferences with project schools. Some twenty-five schools and a hundred teachers had an input into these discussions.

Phase 3

This involved working with our 'research schools' to test out and elaborate the authenticity of the conditions. We used the opportunity of working with these schools on their own teaching and learning agenda to subject our tentative set of conditions to critical and practical scrutiny. At the same time, we also attempted to elaborate in a more academic way the credibility of these conditions for the enhancement of classroom practice by:

- reviewing the relevant research literature
- searching for conceptual clarity
- developing research methods
- creating staff development activities.

Classroom conditions

This is, in no particular order, the list of classroom conditions that has emerged from the three phases of the project:

- *Authentic relationships* – the quality, openness and congruence of relationships existing in the classroom.
- *Boundaries and expectations* – the pattern of expectations set by the teacher and school of student performance and behaviour within the classroom.
- *Planning for teaching* – the access of teachers to a range of pertinent teaching materials and the ability to plan and differentiate these materials for a range of students.
- *Teaching repertoire* – the range of teaching styles and models available for use by a teacher, dependent on student, context, curriculum and desired outcome.
- *Pedagogic partnerships* – the ability of teachers to form professional relationships within and outside the classroom that focus on the study and improvement of practice.
- *Reflection on teaching* – the capacity of the individual teacher to reflect on his or her own practice, and to put to the test of practice, specifications of teaching from other sources.

Towards effective teaching

Recent years have seen considerable media attention given to the question of how teaching can be made more effective. Perhaps stimulated by this publicity, some members of the community, particularly politicians, have been on the lookout for 'quick-fix' responses. In the context of this highly charged debate, a variety of what appear to be easily implemented reforms have been recommended as a means of improving the effectiveness of teaching. These have included suggestions such as more whole-class teaching based on approaches said to be successful in South East Asia, a return to organising classes on the basis of ability, more emphasis on teaching so-called basic skills, and reductions (or, even, increases) in class sizes. Despite the apparent attractions of such approaches, particularly to those who, for whatever reason, want to demonstrate rapid improvement, all carry with them a somewhat simplistic view of the dynamics of classroom interactions. To quote an old Roman historian, they all seem to perceive teaching as being about 'filling empty pots' rather than 'lighting fires'.

There is a central dilemma that faces any teacher faced with a class. Put simply it is this: *how do I work with the whole group and, at the same time, reach out to each member of the class as an individual?* In the years since the right to educational opportunity was extended to all members of the community, it has become increasingly apparent that traditional forms of schooling are no longer adequate for the task. Faced with increased diversity, including the presence of pupils whose cultural experience or even language may be different from their own, and others who may find difficulties in learning within conventional arrangements, teachers have had to think about how they should respond.

Broadly speaking there seem to be three options:

- Continue to maintain the status quo in the belief that those members of the class who do not respond have some 'problem' that prevents their participation.
- Make compromises by reducing expectations in the belief that some pupils will simply never be able to achieve traditional standards.
- Seek to develop new teaching responses that can stimulate and support the participation of all class members.

The problem with the first option, maintaining the status quo, is that it is likely to lead to conflict with some pupils and, possibly, their parents. It may also damage the working atmosphere for everybody, thus making life more stressful for the teacher. The second option, making compromises, involves a reduction in standards, not least for some pupils who may already be vulnerable in our increasingly competitive society. The third option, demanding as it is, has the potential to bring about improvements that can enhance the learning of all pupils whilst at the same time reaching out to those who otherwise have been marginalised.

So, what kinds of practices might help teachers to 'reach out' to all members of the class? What does research suggest about how teachers might develop their practice in order to make it more inclusive? Clearly these are major questions far beyond the scope of this short book. On the other hand, our observations and discussions with pupils and staff in the IQEA Project schools point to some ideas that, at the very least, are worthy of attention.

We notice, for example, that teachers who appear to be effective in providing experiences that facilitate the participation of all members of the class, whilst they each have their own style of working, do pay attention to certain key aspects of classroom life. First of all they seem to recognise that the initial stages of any lesson or activity are particularly important if pupils are to be helped to understand the purpose and meaning of what is to occur. Specifically, they aim to help their pupils to recall previous experiences and knowledge to which new learning can be connected. As one teacher put it, 'I have to warm the class up – I need hot learners not cold learners.'

It is noticeable too the way that more effective teachers use available resources in order to stimulate and support participation. Most significantly, they seem to be aware that the two most important resources for learning are themselves and their pupils. The idea of using the potential of pupils as a resource to one another seems to be a particularly powerful strategy but regrettably in some classrooms it is one that is largely overlooked. Certainly, in our experience, a striking feature of lessons that encourage participation is the way in which pupils are often asked to think aloud, sometimes with the class as a whole as a result of the teacher's sensitive questioning, or with their classmates in well-managed small group situations. All of these provide opportunities for pupils to clarify their own ideas as they 'think aloud', whilst, at the same time, enabling members of the class to stimulate and support one another's learning.

A further noticeable feature of lessons that seem to be successful in reaching all members of the class is the different ways in which pupils are required to engage actively with ideas and materials, and given plenty of opportunities to practise newly acquired skills. Often all of this is encouraged by the setting of problem-solving tasks, carefully planned in order to encourage, indeed require, exploration and application of what is being taught. Problem-solving tasks may be carried out as a whole class, individually or in small working groups. In fact it can be argued that the deliberate use of a variety of contexts is in itself an important means of responding to pupil diversity.

Finally, we find that those lessons we take to be more effective in achieving participation provide frequent opportunities for pupils to reflect upon what occurs in order to clarify emerging understandings. A typical day in school provides pupils with a mass of opportunities and experiences, most of which are rich with possibilities for learning. Unfortunately, in some classrooms little time is made available to allow pupils to reflect upon what they have been doing. In this respect the concluding moments of lessons are particularly critical and should be a time when strategies are used to help pupils to review their learning. Too often we see lessons end abruptly when the teacher suddenly realises that time has run out and things need to be packed away before moving on. Thus, at the key moment when members of the class should be helped to draw their learning together, no time is available.

In the following chapters we provide a range of staff development activities which we hope will address some of these questions and will assist teachers in exploring the classroom conditions for school improvement.

CHAPTER 3

Authentic relationships

We have previously described our findings on the school-level conditions which seem to be most often linked with improvements in the quality of pupil experience (see Hopkins *et al.* 1994, Ainscow *et al.* 1994). As we have continued to explore this area, we have become conscious that it is one thing to recognise that relationships are a major determinant of pupil progress and another to devise strategies that will promote appropriate relationships. This chapter draws on our knowledge of strategies teachers have used to develop quality relationships. In particular, it reflects our experience that authentic relationships between teacher and pupil are promoted when teachers:

    3.1 demonstrate positive regard for all pupils;
    3.2 conduct their relationships in the classroom in ways that demonstrate consistency and fairness and build trust;
    3.3 understand and show that communication with pupils involves listening as much as speaking;
    3.4 make their classrooms places where pupils can safely experiment with behaviours involving choice, risk-taking and personal responsibility.

Overview

Many studies of effective schooling have indicated that the teacher–student relationship is at the heart of the learning process. This is not simply a philosophic proposition emerging from a belief in equity, particularly with regard to the relative rights and obligations of teachers and learners, but a practical contributor to effective classrooms. Consequently, it is a theme which continually appears in writings on effective classrooms. Brandes and Ginnis (1990) indicate that behaviour and commitment improve when (*inter alia*) teachers treat students fairly and with respect, work to build up cooperative and supportive relationships, demonstrate concern for students' needs and welfare and give students meaningful responsibilities within the learning partnership. The essence of this high quality relationship which teachers create within their classrooms is described as 'unconditional positive regard':

The most enabling quality that one person can display to another is unconditional positive regard, a phrase which describes the clear, non-possessive, non-manipulative attitude which seeks the growth and empowerment of the other . . . neither submissive nor subordinate, nor superior, but aligned with the students in following their endeavours and achieving the goals of the school.

(Brandes and Ginnis 1990)

However, descriptions of what a high quality relationship involves are harder to find than exhortations that such relationships are important. The notion that the relationship between pupil and teacher is at the centre of the learning process is by no means new. Indeed, as long ago as 1963, Hook suggested that the teacher must develop a *positive attitude of imaginative concern* for the needs of pupils; Peters (1974) called for close personal relationships with individual learners, advocating *receptiveness and outgoingness* towards each as individual human beings. For Buber (1970), the teacher needed to develop '*Umfassung*', a state through which the teacher, understanding both himself and the pupil, helps the pupil to learn by acting almost as a 'medium' through which knowledge and experience can be transmitted to the learner. Carl Rogers' work in psychology and education also supports this notion; see, for example, his *Freedom to Learn* (Rogers 1983). In this and other publications Rogers identifies some conditions that facilitate *learning to be free*, such as a trust in the human organism, realness in the teacher, unconditional acceptance and empathy.

This is not simply a philosophic proposition emerging from a belief in equity in regard to the relative rights and obligations of teachers and learners. It is a theme which continually appears in writings on effective classrooms. Gray (in Gray and Wilcox 1995), for example, includes as one of his three 'Sheffield Performance Indicators', the opportunity for a student to establish a 'vital' relationship with an adult whilst in school.

Within the IQEA Project schools there have been extended programmes of classroom observation which suggest that a similar emphasis needs to be given to the teacher–pupil relationship. In our own work, we have referred to this as the need to establish *authentic relationships* within the classroom. By this we mean establishing the classroom as a safe and secure learning environment in which pupils can expect acceptance, respect and even warmth from their teachers, without having to earn these – they are intrinsic rights which are extended to pupils because they are there. But beyond this, of course, the security and the mutual trust within the relationship will mean that the teacher is able to make *demands* on the pupils, because there is also *support*.

As might be expected, within the project schools the extent to which this condition is established varies between schools, between classes within the same school, between teachers and even with the same teacher when paired with different teaching groups. Nevertheless, there has been a general acceptance that the schools and the teachers should attempt to extend the *authenticity* of relationships to as many teacher–pupil groups as possible.

Context

In their book *The Student-Centred School* (1990), Donna Brandes and Paul Ginnis suggest that 'The most enabling quality that one person can display to another is unconditional positive regard.'

We have been reminded of that phrase very often in our observations of teachers and classrooms, as we have seen how important the 'messages' teachers give to their pupils are for the development of confidence, self-esteem and personal identity within the classroom. Sometimes, unfortunately, it is a lack of positive regard that is most striking – the (albeit implicit) assumption that pupils must do something to earn the acceptance or approval of the teacher. But on other occasions we have seen how powerful a factor in teacher–pupil relations can be the mutual acceptance and toleration of individual differences. We have tried therefore in our work with schools to promote the view that the pupil, in the first instance at least, fulfils his or her part of the learning contract simply by being there – what happens next is determined by and the responsibility of the teacher. Showing acceptance of pupils and having specific strategies for communicating positive regard to them are accordingly important determinants of classroom relationships.

Briefing

Aims

- To encourage staff to reflect on their own methods of communicating positive acceptance to pupils.
- To provide a 'checklist' of possible strategies as a basis for comparison.
- To focus teacher attention on possible 'new' or 'additional' strategies which could be tried to enhance the quality of classroom relationships.

Process

This activity is organised into three distinct steps. In Step 1, participants are asked to list any methods they currently use to make their pupils feel welcome to and valued within their classes. They are invited to describe briefly how they do this, and then to compare their response with that of a colleague. In Step 2, a list of teacher behaviours which have proved to have a positive impact on teacher–pupil relations is distributed (facilitators should copy the table in Step 2 of Activity 3.1 for distribution) and the pairs are invited to review their own lists in light of these. In Step 3, members of the pairs are asked to help one another to identify one or more strategies for developing current practice, which individuals then write up as personal targets.

Step 1

- Think about your current strategies for making pupils feel welcome in your classroom and positive about themselves as learners.

- Make brief notes on four strategies that you use regularly, identifying if possible when you last used the strategy, with whom and your feelings about its effect.

1.

2.

3.

4.

- Join with a colleague and compare strategies. Spend ten minutes explaining your strategies to your partner and then reverse roles.

Step 2

- This list shows a range of strategies which teachers can use to show their regard for pupils. Which of them do you use? How often? Are there some that you never use? Why?

- Compare your comments with your colleague's.

© IQEA – *Creating the Conditions for Classroom Improvement*

	(Teacher) Behaviour	Comments
A	Called pupils by first names as they entered class	
B	Achieved eye contact with pupils during lesson	
C	Used humour positively	
D	Moved around class and approached all pupils	
E	Attributed ownership of ideas to initiating pupils	
F	Responded positively to incorrect answers, identifying correct parts	
G	Discouraged pupil–pupil verbal abuse	
H	Allowed short breaks where pupils moved about	
I	Organised break when pupils' energy waned	
J	Conveyed sense of enthusiasm in presentation of task	
K	Used anecdotes and/or asides relating to task	
L	Attributed pupils' successes to their efforts	
M	Specified what pupils did to achieve success	
N	Specified expected pupil performance on tasks	

Derived from Marzano *et al.* (1992), *Dimensions of Learning*, Teachers' Manual, Aurora: ASCD/McREL

Step 3

Identify *three* ways that you can develop your current practice. For each, try to identify what the behaviour will require of you, which is different from your current practice, and how you will evaluate whether or not it improves classroom relationships.

Behaviour 1:
I will need to change . . .

Evaluation criteria

Behaviour 2:
I will need to change . . .

Evaluation criteria

Behaviour 3:
I will need to change . . .

Evaluation criteria

Activity 3.2: demonstrating consistency and fairness

Context

Good and Brophy (1980) remind us that pupils expect teachers to do 'what needs doing' and to 'do what they say'. They go on to argue that teachers' credibility with the teaching group is inextricably linked to the consistency and fairness they display in their dealings with the pupils, both as individuals and with the group as a whole.

Our own work reinforces this impression – indeed we would add from our own observations of and discussions with pupils that without a sense of confidence in these qualities pupils rarely develop trust for their teacher. Conversely, we have noted that where pupil–teacher relationships are poor, pupils make frequent reference to their perception that the teacher is 'unfair' or does not deal consistently with particular pupils or behaviour. It is therefore fundamental to classroom relationships that teachers possess these qualities and, equally important, demonstrate them in their day-to-day dealings with pupils.

Briefing

Aims

- To help teachers to focus on the factors which contribute to or reduce pupils' perception of fairness and consistency from teachers.
- To encourage teachers to compare their views with views compiled from a survey of pupils.
- To help teachers to reflect on an occasion when they have not behaved in a way likely to increase trust and learn from this.

Process

This activity is organised in three steps. Step 1 asks participants individually, and then in small groups, to identify factors which undermine teacher–pupil relationships. This should be completed before Step 2 is issued. Step 2 includes a list drawn from pupils, which can be used as a checklist to compare with the lists emerging from the first stage. Step 3 asks teachers to think back over an instance where their judgement was not the best. It involves reviewing the situation in discussion with a colleague and identifying lessons to be learned.

Step 1

• What do you think spoils the development of trust between pupils and teachers? Make a list of the factors you think undermine pupils' trust in their teachers.

Factors undermining trust

• Join with two colleagues and compare your lists. You should try to agree as a group on the *six* teacher behaviours which are most likely to be interpreted as 'unfair' by pupils and reduce levels of trust.

1.

2.

3.

4.

5.

6.

© IQEA – *Creating the Conditions for Classroom Improvement*

Step 2

The following list is derived from a survey of pupils' views on what makes it hard to 'trust' a teacher:

- not following through on promises

- not helping when you really need help

- never admitting they were wrong

- punishing everyone when they don't know who is to blame

- not punishing their 'favourite' pupils

- making threats

- 'silly' rules (such as 'don't leave your desk'!)

- rules they don't follow themselves

- not giving everyone 'a chance'.

How does it compare with your own list?

Step 3

- Can you (individually) identify an occasion when you feel that the way you handled the situation reduced teacher–pupil trust? Briefly describe it.

- Pair with a colleague and exchange accounts. What can you learn from this that is likely to help you in future relationships with pupils?

Activity 3.3: developing listening skills

Context

The quality of classroom communication has a major influence on the way pupils feel about their experience in that classroom. Just as it is important that teachers are clear in giving instructions or conveying their feelings to pupils, it is important that pupils feel the teacher is equally sensitive to what they are saying. We have noticed in our observations of classrooms that teachers are frequently very alert to what is happening in the classroom and may even be adept at tuning into conversations between pupils. However, this 'awareness' of what pupils are saying is not always reflected in the teacher's communication with pupils. Indeed, often it seems that the teacher is monitoring pupil talk rather than responding to it, even where the talk is addressed directly to the teacher. The activity is intended to help teachers to think about their own listening skills, first of all in general terms and then specifically in relation to classroom practice.

Briefing

Aims

- To give teachers an opportunity to practise their 'listening skills', and to consider what are the features of effective listening.
- To help teachers to reflect on the extent to which they use their listening skills within the classroom and to develop specific ideas about how to use these more effectively.

Process

This activity is organised in five steps. The first three relate to a 'listening skills' exercise, which requires a set of cards for each group. The facilitator should identify the groups, 'deal' the cards amongst group members, asking them not to look at the cards until the instructions have been read to them, then read out the instruction sheet. Groups should be given about 10 to 15 minutes to solve the problem, then moved onto Step 2, a discussion of what they have been doing. In Step 3 groups share their conclusions. In Step 4 participants work in small groups to identify behaviours they can use in the classroom that signal to pupils that they are listened to, and the activity closes in Step 5 with a sharing of ideas about how teachers might show active listening to their pupils.

Step 1

This exercise requires the participants to be organised into groups of five or six members. A set of cards is required for each participating group.

Cards for Step 1 – copy one set for each group.

It is 7 flipz from Ainscow to Beresford	
	A tokz is 8 tikz

Statements to be printed on cards:

- It is 7 flipz from Ainscow to Beresford.
- It is 11 flipz from Beresford to Harris.
- It is 2 flopz from Harris to Hopkins.
- There are 8 flipz in a flopz.
- A flipz is a measure of distance.
- There are 4 flopz in a country mile.
- A tokz is 8 tikz.
- A minim is 2 tokz.
- A minim is a unit of time.
- Tokz and tikz are measures of time.
- Jack sets out at midday.
- A minim equals 4 hours.
- Jack drives from Ainscow to Beresford at a speed of 28 flipz per tikz.
- Jack drives from Beresford to Harris at a speed of 22 flipz per tikz.
- Jack drives from Harris to Hopkins at a speed of 32 flipz per tikz.
- The shortest route between Ainscow and Hopkins is 3 flopz.

The facilitator should organise the groups and distribute the cards amongst group members, giving the following instructions (*verbally*) to groups.

Instruction sheet

1. The task for each group is to solve a problem.

2. The information needed to solve the problem is written on the cards they have before them.

3. Each member of the group is responsible for his/her own cards.

4. Group members may tell each other what is written on their cards, but must not show or transfer these to any other group member.

5. No pens or paper are allowed during the exercise which must be solved by speaking and listening.

6. All groups have the same cards.

7. The problem to be solved is: To the nearest minute, how long did the journey from Ainscow to Hopkins take Jack, if he drove via Beresford and Harris without stopping?

Step 2   Remaining in groups, spend ten minutes reflecting on the way the group tackled the problem. Consider:

- What behaviour helped the group?

- What behaviour hindered the group?

- Who participated most? Why do you think this was?

- Who participated least? Why do you think this was?

- How did leadership emerge in the group?

- What were your feelings as the activity progressed?

Step 3   • Share your conclusions with the whole group.

   • What can we learn about effective listening from this exercise?

Step 4

In small groups (three or four members) make a list of six behaviours that teachers can adopt to demonstrate to pupils that they listen to what they say.

Demonstrating active listening

1.

2.

3.

4.

5.

6.

Step 5

Share your list with the whole group.

Activity 3.4: encouraging choice and risk-taking

Context

It is well established that an effective learning environment is one in which the learner is encouraged to take responsibility for his or her own learning. However, 'taking responsibility' implies the availability of choices (unless we are simply creating a 'blame culture' to transfer accountability away from teachers). It is through exercising choices which influence the patterns of experience and provide opportunities to experiment with new behaviours that pupils can come to understand that growth and risk-taking are frequently to be found together. They can also experience how making a choice implies an acceptance of the outcomes of that choice – although there may not always be the hoped-for outcomes. Indeed, any genuine empowerment of pupils brings with it the possibility that we will allow them to experience failure. But it should be failure which is itself seen as an important learning experience, since without the possibility of failure there may be little opportunity for real development. In this sense, the classroom needs to be a place where pupils can fail safely, learn from poor choices and be encouraged to grow through that experience. This exercise invites teachers to reflect upon the extent to which their own pupils are encouraged to experiment with behaviours, to make choices, and what strategies are available to help pupils come through occasional failures strengthened by the experience.

Briefing

Aims

- To analyse recent teaching to see how far the possibility of pupils making choices about their own learning exists.
- To consider, with colleagues, how pupil choice can be increased.
- To consider ways of using negative outcome from pupil choice as a positive learning experience.

Process

This activity is divided into four steps. Step 1 requires participants to work alone, reflecting on their most recent teaching experience, then describing this to colleagues. The relevant sheet should be copied for each participant and given out for completion before Step 2 is issued. Step 3 allows the participants to act as a resource to one another, and in Step 4 the whole group is invited to pool its ideas on how teachers can make positive use of experiences which may not seem so positive for individual students at the time.

Step 1

- Make a list of the last six lessons you have taught, briefly setting out the content, the teaching method(s) and indicating the class or group.

	Content description	Method description
Lesson 1 Class/group:		
Lesson 2 Class/group:		
Lesson 3 Class/group:		
Lesson 4 Class/group:		
Lesson 5 Class/group:		
Lesson 6 Class/group:		

- Join with two colleagues. Briefly (five minutes each) take turns to describe your 'methods' to one another.

© IQEA – *Creating the Conditions for Classroom Improvement*

Step 2

- Reviewing the six lessons you have described, go through each one in turn noting any opportunities you provided for the pupils to make choices about the content or the methods of the lesson.

	Choices available	
	Content	**Method**
Lesson 1		
Lesson 2		
Lesson 3		
Lesson 4		
Lesson 5		
Lesson 6		

- Regroup with your two colleagues and compare responses.

Step 3

Staying in threes, look again at Step 2. Can you help each other to identify opportunities to build pupil choice into the lessons described?

Step 4

- Still as a group of three, think for ten minutes about how pupil failure can be used positively as a learning experience. Select two examples.

---

1. Failure can be used positively when . . .

2. Failure can be used positively when . . .

- Share your two examples with the whole group.

CHAPTER 4

Boundaries and expectations

It is apparent from our observations of practice that where teachers act in concert, demonstrating similar ranges of approaches and behaviours, these patterns are learned quickly by students, who then recognise them as cues. Nowhere is this more evident than in the expectations of students' behaviour. Consistent adherence to an announced code is an important determinant of student response. Where rules are clearly set out and faithfully followed, most students seem to learn very quickly to function within the boundaries these establish.

It is equally apparent that the expectations teachers hold of pupil behaviour, as well as participation and commitment, are grounded within their established boundaries. Within the IQEA Project schools, we have seen that teacher and pupil expectations increase as the classroom environment becomes a physically and emotionally secure space. Specifically, we have noted that the creation of a purposeful learning environment seems most often to be associated with:

4.1 clear boundaries to, and expectations of, pupil behaviour;
4.2 a system of rewards and sanctions that emphasises expectations and promotes pupil self-esteem and self-discipline;
4.3 active classroom management strategies aimed at creating and maintaining an appropriate classroom environment;
4.4 consistency, without inflexibility, in responding to pupils and events.

Overview   If we hope pupils will value and enjoy learning, we need to be able to create a learning environment in which pupils will feel secure and valued. In the previous chapter, we noted that relationships are central to the pupils' sense of self-esteem and progress within the classroom. But relationships are often stunted by problems arising from discipline or control problems. It is ironic, but inescapable, that the level of individual freedom within the classroom will be tied to the observance of 'rules'. Unless some rules or boundaries are observed by all pupils, there will be little opportunity for any pupil to act individually or creatively. Boundaries to pupil behaviour are therefore necessary, not to restrict pupils but to release them. It is important therefore that the classroom has 'rules' – positively stated, explained to pupils, discussed and negotiated when appropriate, but consistently applied.

There are obvious side benefits to clearly articulated and consistently enforced rules: for example, the level of support these offer to the teacher who is comparatively weak. But the main impact seems to be on the classroom climate, and therefore on the possibility of developing the other classroom conditions we address in this book. Because of this, the clarification of classroom 'rules' and expectations benefits individual teachers by contributing to the quality of the learning environment. Collective agreement and consistent behaviour across teachers is a very potent influence indeed on student response, so where possible differences between teachers should be avoided. This, in turn, argues for a minimum of necessary 'rules', since the more there are, the harder it will be to secure agreement and coordinate the responses of teachers.

It is also important to see the boundaries that are set for pupils as positive expectations, rather than as strategies for control *per se*. Ultimately, the hope is that pupils will be self-controlling within the set boundaries, and that the expectations of teachers can then be addressed towards more challenging outcomes from their pupils than simple compliance.

Of course, the method through which appropriate *boundaries* are identified is, in itself, an important reinforcer of the *boundaries*. Our experience suggests that where the limits on pupil and teacher behaviour are arrived at through a process of 'negotiation' – that is one which involves the students themselves and reflects their views – there is a much deeper commitment to observe these limits.

Activity 4.1: establishing boundaries

Context

The reason schools need rules is to create a physically and psychologically safe environment for teaching and learning. Rules are recognised, even by quite young children, as necessary components of the learning environment, and sensible rules facilitate effective and efficient classroom management, maximising the amount of time pupils spend on learning activities. However, since 'rules' are intended to be supportive of the educational aims and processes of the school, it follows that rules which are not necessary for these purposes, or that reduce levels of pupil commitment or morale, should be avoided. Generally, rules need to be accepted to be effective and are required to meet a need to be accepted. It is important therefore to keep rules to a minimum and to try to ground them in principles which safeguard and promote the pupils' interests. It is also important to ensure that the minimum of rules, once adopted, command support from and are acted on by all teachers – nothing so discredits school rules as varying levels of implementation.

This activity is designed to help teachers explore their own thinking about necessary rules in schools and the interaction between rules, expectations and pupil behaviour.

Briefing

Aims

- To help teachers to reflect on the purposes served by 'rules' in school.
- To provide an opportunity to review their own school's practices regarding 'rule-making'.
- To help teachers to consider how 'rules' might be 'taught' to their pupils.

Process

This activity is conducted in five steps. For Steps 1 and 2, participants will need to bring a copy of their own school rules. Facilitators should also make copies of the 'rules' from the other sector (primary or secondary) for comparison purposes. For Steps 2 and 3, copies of the relevant lists (A and B) will be needed.

Step 1

- Consider the rules from the school in the other sector. Read these individually and make any brief notes you wish.

- Join with two colleagues and together compare these sets of rules with the rules from your own school.

What are the main similarities/differences?

What do you feel the rules tell you about the culture of the school from which they come?

© IQEA – *Creating the Conditions for Classroom Improvement*

Are there any modifications you would like to make to your own school's rules?

Step 2

- Here are some 'criteria' for assessing the appropriateness of school rules.

LIST A

The rule should be needed.

The rule should be reasonable.

The rule should be simple and clear.

The rule should be flexible.

Where possible, the rule should be expressed positively.

The rule should be appropriate to the levels of cognitive and social development of the pupils.

- Do you agree with this list?

- How well do your own school's rules stand up to these criteria?

Step 3

- The procedures used to develop and publish rules are likely to have a clear influence on the extent to which pupils accept rules as 'expectations' of behaviour. It is recommended that the following procedures be followed if rules are to have maximum impact.

LIST B

Rules should be drawn up before the school year starts.

Rules should be displayed around the school.

Pupils should have copies of the rules.

The consequences of breaking rules should be clear.

There should be a minimum number of rules.

Schools should 'teach' rules.

- How far would you agree with these procedures?
- Does your own school's practice reflect these procedures?

Step 4

- Choose *one* rule from your own school which is proving difficult to enforce.
- How might you 'teach' the rule to pupils?

Step 5

Report back to the whole group on the teaching strategy you have devised.

Activity 4.2: using discipline positively

Context

Although it is true that effective teachers behave in an authoritarian manner when they perceive the need to give direct guidance or to intervene, few effective teachers behave in this way all the time. Requests, suggestions, reminders are often equally effective in securing the cooperation of pupils, and they at the same time contribute to a more positive classroom climate – a climate of mutual purpose and regard. Indeed, it is characteristic of effective teachers that they offer a classroom in which pupils are encouraged to grow and to learn, yet also one in which there is clear direction and, when necessary, control. Such teachers recognise that discipline needs to be used as a positive force in the classroom, not a means of repression. But, if rewards and sanctions are to be harnessed as methods to promote the pupils' sense of self-worth and to encourage self-discipline, the teacher needs to be aware of and skilled in reflecting from a wide range of discipline strategies.

Briefing

Aims

- To help teachers to reflect on their own use of punishments/sanctions.
- To promote discussion about the efficiency of particular sanctions with regard to particular problems.
- To remind teachers of the range of behaviours available when they seek to intervene and redirect pupil behaviour.
- To identify ways in which discipline can be used as a positive force within the school.

Process

This activity is organised in four steps. Step 1 invites teachers to reflect upon their own (recent) use of punishments or sanctions, identifying why they were used and what was achieved. Colleagues are then asked to compare responses. In Step 2 each participant is asked to focus more closely on a particular incident which is recurring or causing trouble, and to think in more detail about this linking of punishment and behaviour. Colleagues then act as 'consultants' to one another, suggesting alternative strategies. Step 3 involves the matching of teacher response with pupil behaviour, and is intended to be carried out as a small group exercise. Step 4 involves pairs of teachers, reflecting on why certain types of problem persist, certain punishments seem to have little effect, and asks the pairs to 'brainstorm' ways of making the discipline system of the school more positive.

Step 1   Make a list of five punishments/sanctions you have used in the last week with various classes. Identify why they were used and what was achieved. Put this information in the following matrix.

Sanction/ punishment	Reason	Outcome

Step 2   With a colleague share your responses. Focus particularly upon the nature of the incident and the appropriateness of the sanction/punishment. Are some sanctions/punishments more important than others, why, why not? Make some notes of your conversation.

Step 3   In small groups elaborate your responses by matching sanction/punishment to pupil behaviour. Make a list of typical pupil misbehaviours and those sanctions/punishments that most match the degree of the misbehaviour. Put these group lists around the room and spend some time reading all the group lists.

Step 4   With a colleague use the lists to consider why certain pupil behaviours still persist despite well-matched sanctions/punishments. Discuss whether there are any other ways of addressing the persistent behaviour problem than currently exist. What might need to happen in order for new strategies to be fully accepted and implemented?

Activity 4.3: creating and maintaining an appropriate classroom environment

Context

It is clear from our research that classroom seating arrangements are important factors in effective teaching and learning. This, perhaps, has been more readily recognised in the primary sector than in the secondary one. Yet in secondary schools it is apparent, when talking in particular to students in Years 8 and 9, that where you sit in class is a reflection of your status outside the classroom, as well as being a contributory factor to the maintenance of that status. Students in all years characterise the traditional system of desks in rows as 'trouble-makers at the back, workers in the middle and sad people with no friends at the front'. Moving a disruptive student from the back row to the front upsets this classroom social structure, and thus can cause even greater disruption than the original incident.

Such a powerful image of the learning environment inevitably has some impact upon the teaching processes in the classroom, yet our research suggests that secondary teachers pay little heed to seating arrangements. They seem content to accept the arrangement they find when they enter a room. The students we questioned, although holding forceful views about various seating arrangements, were content to allow the teacher to dictate the seating arrangements. This state of 'stasis by default' often means that teachers deploy teaching strategies, such as groupwork, in utterly inappropriate situations.

Briefing

Aims

- To devise a seating arrangement for the classroom to meet the teaching needs of the teacher and the learning needs of the students.
- To consider how the views of students can be incorporated into the arrangement.
- To consider how particular types of students can be integrated into the arrangement.

Process

This activity is divided into five steps. Step 1 requires participants to consider alone the optimum seating arrangement for a particular class they teach. Step 2 involves them discussing with a partner how student views on classroom seating arrangements can be sought. Step 3 presents them with a seating arrangement preferred by the students but different from their own, and Step 4 requires them to discuss with the same partner ways to reconcile the difference. Lastly, views are shared with the rest of the group.

Step 1   In the space below, draw a plan of how you would prefer the seating to be arranged when you are teaching a particular class. Locate particular types of students, especially those you deem disruptive and those the rest of the class describe as 'boffs', by initialling their table places.

Blackboard

Step 2

- With a partner, devise a way of canvassing the views of the students in the class.

- What are the key questions you would ask?

- How could you integrate your own views on your teaching requirements into the enquiry?

1.

2.

3.

4.

5.

6.

Step 3	The class has come out heavily in favour of a seating arrangement different from the one you devised in Step 1. If your preference was to seat the class in rows, the students have come out in favour of sitting in groups of four around two tables. If you favoured a horseshoe arrangement, they have expressed a wish to sit in rows. If you wished to sit them in groups, they wish to sit in rows.

Step 4	• With the same partner as for Step 2, devise a strategy for reconciling the two different versions.
	• Would you bow to the students' preference?
	• Would you impose yours?

Step 5	Share your views with the rest of the group.

Activity 4.4: consistency, without inflexibility, in responding to pupils and events

Context

It is generally accepted that effective classrooms are characterised by a positive working atmosphere which includes an emphasis on celebrating achievement. Providing feedback to pupils as they carry out their tasks and giving praise for effort and achievement are essential to the creation of such an atmosphere. It is important, however, to recognise that praise is a complex social process. Too often teachers have been asked to believe that simply increasing the use of praise will lead to improvements in learning and social behaviour. At its worst this leads to a mechanistic approach within which praise is offered as a largely manipulative strategy. It is important, therefore, to explore the features of appropriate forms of praise.

Research suggests that effective praise draws attention to progress and achievement, while at the same time expressing appreciation for the pupil's efforts in ways that indicate a recognition for their own value rather than their role in pleasing the teacher. This helps pupils to attribute their achievements to their own intrinsic motivation rather than to external manipulation by the teacher, lack of challenge in the task or sheer luck.

Briefing

Aim

• To examine how praise should be used.

Process

During Step 1 participants consider research evidence, seeking to relate this to their own ideas and experiences. Then, at Step 2, groups develop guidelines that are relevant to the pupils within the school. Finally, the groups share and compare their proposals.

© IQEA – *Creating the Conditions for Classroom Improvement*

Step 1

Following an initial discussion based on the context material, participants are asked to consider in small groups the following list of statements based on a summary of the findings of research. Discussion should be focused on two issues in respect to each statement, i.e. What does this statement mean? Do we agree with this idea?

Effective praise should:

- be simple and direct, delivered in a natural voice, without gushing or dramatising

- be in a straightforward, declarative style (e.g. 'That's interesting, I never thought of that before')

- specify the particular accomplishment, recognising any noteworthy effort, care or perseverance

- be varied

- be backed with appropriate nonverbal communication

- avoid ambiguous statements (e.g. 'You were really good today')

- usually be expressed privately.

Step 2

Groups are asked to develop their own guidelines on effective ways of celebrating pupil efforts and achievements. Their ideas should be summarised on a flipchart.

Step 3

Each group presents its ideas using the flipchart displays, and this is followed by discussion.

Step 4   Participants write a memo as follows:

The most important thing about praise is . . .

© IQEA – *Creating the Conditions for Classroom Improvement*

CHAPTER 5

Planning for teaching

The planning of lessons and, indeed, activities within lessons, is of course central to the success of teaching. Inexperienced teachers have to plan their work in considerable detail, starting from the goals of the curriculum and the syllabus in order to formulate opportunities, experiences and materials that will facilitate the learning of their pupils. On the other hand, more experienced teachers are often able to formulate their plans from a range of possibilities within their existing repertoire, which they adapt in response to the situation faced. Thus, planning becomes an on-going process of adaptation based on the teacher's reading of the needs of their pupils. The skills involved in this kind of planning are developed through professional experience.

Our observation is that the impact of the many hours teachers spend preparing their lessons is increased when:

5.1 variety is built into lesson plans;
5.2 classroom arrangements are adjusted in response to pupil feedback during lessons;
5.3 strategies are planned to enable pupils to find meaning in lesson activities;
5.4 homework is planned in order to reinforce and extend learning.

Overview   During initial training, student teachers are usually introduced to systematic planning procedures that require them to have lesson outlines describing objectives, methods, materials and forms of evaluation to be used. For inexperienced teachers this provides a framework for thinking about the factors that may well influence the success of the lesson and, at the same time, a means of anticipating possible difficulties. Unfortunately, classroom life is full of possibilities for the unexpected to occur and while many lessons follow a somewhat predictable overall pattern, they also involve numerous unforeseen minor events that have to be addressed. Consequently, even a well-planned lesson in the hands of an inexperienced practitioner can lead to frustrations, as potentially rich opportunities for extending learning are overlooked, or distracting incidents allowed to damage the climate of the classroom.

Our own observations of planning processes used by more effective teachers suggest that different, more flexible procedures are usually at work. Often experienced teachers have developed a range of lesson formats that become their repertoire and from which they create arrangements that they judge to be appropriate to a particular purpose. Here they seem to take account of a range of interconnected factors, such as the subject to be taught, the age and experience of the class, the environmental conditions of the classroom, the available resources and their own mood, in order to adapt one of their usual lesson outlines. Such planning tends to be rather idiosyncratic and, indeed, often seems to be conducted at a largely intuitive level. In this sense it is unlike the rather rationale procedure introduced to novices in that it consists, to a large degree, of an on-going process of designing and redesigning established patterns.

Much of this planning, therefore, goes on incidentally in the background as teachers go about their day-to-day business. Whilst some of it may occur over the weekend or in the evening, it also continues on the way to school in the morning and on into the building as the teacher gathers things together for the lesson. Indeed it sometimes strikes us that final adjustments are still being made as the teacher enters the classroom and judges the mood of the class.

All of this may sound rather informal, even hit and miss, but our observations indicate that for many experienced teachers it involves an intellectually demanding process of self-dialogue about how best to stimulate the learning of the class. Attempts to encourage and support further improvements in practice in this area must, therefore, take account of the nature of this complex approach to planning.

There is a rather obvious limitation to this approach to classroom planning that arises from the largely private way in which it is conducted. This means that the teacher is confined to the range of possibilities that is suggested from earlier experiences. This is why within the IQEA Project schools are encouraged to develop organisational conditions that lead to discussions of teaching and sharing of experiences about how lessons might be planned (see Ainscow *et al.* 1994, in particular chapter 7).

It is also essential to recognise that planning does not end when the lesson starts. Indeed, often the most significant decisions are those that are made as the lesson proceeds. In this respect, one researcher compares the work of teachers to that of artisans. An example will illustrate the point he makes. Faced with a leak in a sink an experienced plumber sets about the task in the certain knowledge that he or she has the wherewithal to solve the problem. Since he has fixed many similar leaks before he is confident that one of his usual responses will do the trick. Occasionally, however, he experiences a surprise – his usual repertoire proves to be inadequate. What does he do? Does he go on a course? Call for help? Read a manual? More likely he will tinker with the problem pipes until he is able to invent a solution. In this way he adds a new way of working to his repertoire, which, of course, he can then take with him to the next leaking sink.

The suggestion is that this is something like the way in which teachers develop their practices. Arguably the key difference is that teaching is far less predictable than plumbing; so much so that during each lesson there are many 'surprises' to be dealt with and, therefore, far more possibilities for 'tinkering'. For example, there is the pupil who suddenly wants to tell the teacher about something interesting that happened the previous night; another who asks a question about the subject of the lesson that the teacher has never thought of, and, inevitably, those who lose interest or misbehave in some way. All of these unexpected events require an instant decision. Just like the plumber, the teacher has no opportunity to take advice. In this way new responses are trialled and, where they are found to be of value, added to the teachers' range of usual approaches. Through this form of *planning for teaching*, teachers learn how to plan classroom arrangements that can be more effective in responding to individuals within their classes.

Activity 5.1: planning for variety

Context

The pupils that teachers work with in the schools of today live in a world of interest and excitement. Many have opportunities to travel, while even those who do not are accustomed to a rich diet of stimulation through television, films and computers. In this sense they present challenges not faced by earlier generations of teachers. The pupils of today are, therefore, demanding and discriminating; they also bring to the classroom experiences and ideas that can provide important foundations upon which lessons can be planned.

In another important sense one generation of pupils is much the same as any other. Specifically, any class contains a set of individuals each of which has their own interests, fears and aptitudes. How to prepare for this diversity is at the heart of the planning process.

For all of these reasons a concern with variety is essential to effective planning. If we are to provide schooling that will motivate participation and learning, build upon the varied experiences of members of the class, and take account of the differences of learning style, it is necessary to consider how lessons can be planned in ways that provide a rich range of learning contexts, experiences and materials.

Briefing

Aims

- To encourage staff to consider the nature of diversity within a typical class.
- To explore how variety might be built into a lesson in response to pupil diversity.

Process

Participants should read the introductory text and discuss their thoughts on how variety might be built into lessons. This helps to focus the mind prior to more detailed discussions.

During Step 1, participants work in silence, completing the seven sentences. It may help if the person leading the activity suggests that the group recall their experiences as learners in school or college, or of more recent learning experiences such as when learning to drive a car. This is followed by a period spent talking in pairs, leading to group work in fours or sixes where individuals take turns to explain their ideas. Eventually groups are asked to design and produce a poster. Experience suggests that this way of working encourages groups to consider more closely the ideas presented by individuals.

The 'tour' of the posters forces individuals to articulate the learning that occurred in the earlier groups. In this way it allows for consolidation of learning while, at the same time, encouraging the sharing of ideas. The final step, writing a memo, allows individuals to relate what has happened to their own interests. If there is time, individuals can be invited to read their memos aloud in order to foster yet further discussion.

Step 1   Think about the way you learn. Working on your own, complete these sentences:

Myself as a learner

1. I learn slowly when . . .

2. I learn quickly when . . .

3. I find learning easy when . . .

4. Learning in groups . . .

5. Learning from books . . .

6. I learn well from . . .

7. I enjoy learning when . . .

Step 2   Having completed the sentences, form a partnership with a colleague. Read your sentences and explain what you had in mind.

Step 3

With your partner join one or two other pairs of colleagues. Going round the group, each person explains their ideas. Listen carefully, looking for patterns in what is said. Once everyone has spoken, consider the implications of what you have heard. Specifically, how would a teacher faced with such diversity in the class plan a lesson to take account of the preferences of each individual? As a group, design and produce a poster that will get your recommendations across to other teachers. The poster should be clear, bold and interesting.

Step 4

Place the various posters on the wall around the room. Form new groups in which there is at least one member of each of the old groups. Now 'tour' the room, allowing the member of your group who designed each poster to explain the concept and answer questions.

Step 5

On your own complete the following memo.

In the light of this activity I want to . . .

© IQEA – *Creating the Conditions for Classroom Improvement*

Context

Our observations within schools in the IQEA network suggest that very effective teachers are particularly skilful improvisers. Throughout a lesson they are gauging the reactions of the class to what is happening, noting body language and facial expressions, as well as observing more formally the responses pupils make. Mostly this monitoring goes on at an intuitive level as the teacher juggles with the many tasks and decisions required during the lesson. It is in this way, it seems, that teachers make the adjustments that are necessary in order to encourage the engagement of all class members.

Improvisation can take many forms. For example, it can involve adjustments in timing because some pupils appear bored or distracted; stepping up of pressure in order to stimulate greater effort or a deeper engagement with the topic being considered; individual attention to those who seem to need more support; or clarification of explanations or instructions because there looks to be some uncertainty about the tasks that have been set.

Briefing

Aim

- To encourage participants to reflect about how they improvise during lessons.

Process

Following an introductory discussion about the idea of improvisation in teaching, stimulated by the context-setting text above, participants are given five minutes in which to complete the table. It is helpful to suggest that they should bring to mind a class they have taught recently, thinking in particular about different things that occurred during the lesson and how they reacted.

Step 2 is carried out in pairs, with each person having time to explain their ideas. Here it should be stressed that this is an opportunity to 'think aloud'. The issues under consideration are rather subtle and it is intended that the conversations will enable those involved to get a greater understanding of the basis of their own practice. After a reasonable period the pairs form larger groups so that in Step 3 the discussions can be extended. Finally, during Step 4, individuals are given a few moments to write a personal memo pointing to actions that might be taken.

If possible, it would make sense to follow up these discussions with some form of mutual observation in the classroom in order to explore in more detail the forms of improvisation used by the colleagues involved. Such observations should provide opportunities for teachers to create a common language that can be used to explore aspects of classroom practice.

Step 1   Add your ideas to the following table:

Sometimes I adjust my lesson plans by		
Clarifying instructions		Reviewing understandings
Stepping up pressure		Changing the pace
	Providing individual help	

Step 2   Compare your table with a colleague's. Try to come to an agreement as to which are the three tactics that are most useful.

Step 3   Staying with your partner, form groups of four or six. Share your conclusions.

© IQEA – *Creating the Conditions for Classroom Improvement*

Step 4

In the light of this discussion about ways of adjusting lessons, I intend to . . .

Activity 5.3: finding meaning

Context

Most lessons provide a range of possibilities that can be used to foster learning. Usually teachers have thought carefully about how they might stimulate interest in order to engage the class in the themes of the lesson. Sometimes, however, the full potential of all of this is not achieved. Too often, as T. S. Eliot once remarked, those involved 'had the experience but missed the meaning'. In planning lessons, therefore, it is important to consider how strategies can be built in that will stimulate the personal reflection that can facilitate understanding and learning.

Current thinking in cognitive psychology emphasises the idea that learning is a personal process of 'meaning-making', with each participant in an event constructing their own version of that shared experience. The implication is that even in what might be seen as a rather traditional lesson, with little apparent concession being made by the teacher to the individual differences of members of the class, each pupil experiences and defines the meaning of what occurs in their own way. Interpreting the experience in terms of their own mental frames, individuals construct forms of knowledge which may or may not relate to the purposes and understandings of the teacher.

Recognising this personal process of meaning-making leads the teacher to include in their lesson plans opportunities for self-reflection, in order that pupils can be encouraged to engage with and make a personal record of their own developing understandings.

Briefing

Aim

- To facilitate the sharing of expertise about how strategies might be built into a lesson in order to help pupils find meaning.

Process

Working in groups, Step 1 of the activity involves participants in agreeing common meanings of the ideas on nine cards prepared by the course leader from the nine items listed in the box on the next page. Towards the end of this discussion it may be useful to offer the groups an opportunity to add at least one additional card of their own.

The groups then carry out what is sometimes called the diamond-ranking exercise. This forces the group to come to a consensus. New groups are then formed in order to discuss the conclusions of the various working groups. This approach, known as the jigsaw classroom, illustrates one of the most effective forms of cooperative learning. Its strength is that it encourages all individuals to participate actively, whilst at the same time deepening the level of engagement with the topic under consideration. It is an approach that can easily be adapted for use with pupils.

Finally, in Step 4, there is general discussion, followed by a 'round' during which individuals think aloud about the significance of the activity.

Step 1

Form groups of four. Each group is given a set of nine cards which suggest ways in which members of a class might be helped to find meaning during a lesson. The group first of all considers what each card means.

> **Nine ways in which pupils can be helped to find meaning**
>
> • Writing in an individual learning journal.
>
> • Small group discussions.
>
> • Oral questions to the whole class.
>
> • Brainstorming ideas about the subject of the lesson.
>
> • Individuals designing a visual map of what they think they have learnt.
>
> • Providing examples from everyday life.
>
> • Field trips and projects.
>
> • Role play.
>
> • Making tasks functional.

Step 2

Groups work to arrange the cards into a diamond pattern like this:

```
              1
          2       2
       3      3       3
          4       4
              5
```

The statements should be in priority order, where '1' is of the highest priority and the statement at '5' is the lowest priority idea.

Step 3

Group members are given a number 1 to 4. All participants with the same number form a new group. These new groups move around the room discussing the different diamond arrangements.

Step 4

The whole group discusses the differences it has noted, considering the implications. The activity concludes with a 'round'. This involves each participant completing the following sentence: 'The most interesting thing for me was . . .' It should be stressed that it is acceptable to say 'pass' if they have nothing to say.

Context

Homework can provide opportunities to consolidate and extend the learning that goes on in classrooms. It also provides further opportunities to make connections with experiences outside of school, while, at the same time, encouraging pupils to take more responsibility for their progress. Too often, however, it seems to become a rather purposeless chore, requiring little more than completing tasks for the sake of it!

In order to gain the potential benefits of homework, it is helpful for groups of staff within a school or department to carry out a review of existing practice. A useful starting point for such a review are the findings of a recent HMI survey carried out in primary, middle and secondary schools (i.e. OFSTED 1995, *Homework in Primary and Secondary Schools*, HMSO). The report argues that where homework is 'taken seriously' by staff, pupils and parents it can:

- raise standards
- extend coverage of the curriculum
- make better use of time in lessons
- improve pupils' attitudes to learning
- improve pupils' organisational and study skills.

The activities on the following pages encourage a review that takes account of these possibilities.

Briefing

Aim

- To review existing policies on homework with a view to bringing about improvements in practice.

Process

The activity involves working groups set up to review current practices. The exact format will need to be planned to fit in with the situation in the particular school. So, for example, in a secondary school it would be probably sensible to work in departmental teams, whereas in a primary school it might be better to use key stage teams. Each group analyses at least one pupil's weekly homework. Eventually the groups come together to use their findings as a basis for reviewing overall policy.

Step 1   Working groups are formed to examine homework policy. These may be based on subject specialisms or in relationship to the age group of pupils taught. Each group collects all the homework done by a particular pupil within one week. Time is taken to peruse this material. The group then prepares written answers to the following questions:

- What are the main purposes of the homework?
- In what ways does it contribute to the pupil's learning?
- How varied are the tasks?
- How challenging were the tasks that were set?
- Is there sufficient support for those who may experience difficulties?
- Is the amount of homework appropriate?

Step 2   Each working group presents its findings. These are used to reflect upon current policy with a view to making necessary changes.

CHAPTER 6

Teaching repertoire

Effective teachers have a range of learning activities, tasks or experiences for pupils which they know are successful in bringing about certain types of pupil learning (knowledge, understanding, skills and attitudes). In practice, more effective practitioners have a range of teaching skills, styles, models and approaches which comprise a teaching repertoire. We have noted from our work with IQEA Project schools that effective teaching seems most associated with:

6.1 a range of teaching skills which comprise a teacher's repertoire;

6.2 various teaching styles or approaches which teachers adopt;

6.3 different teaching models which teachers develop and refine;

6.4 the centrality of reflection and the importance of artistry within a teacher's repertoire.

Overview

Powerful learning does not occur by accident but is usually the result of an effective learning situation created by a skilful teacher. It is the conscious linking of teaching to learning irrespective to some extent of curriculum content. In our work we have found that teaching can make a big difference to students both at the classroom and school levels. As Joyce and Showers (1991:12) argue, 'effective teachers are confident that they can make a difference and that the difference is made by increasing their own teaching repertoires and the learning repertoires of their students'.

There are many different perspectives on the theme of quality teaching and teaching repertoires. Hopkins (1997) has suggested that there are three broad aspects to quality teaching that have their own literature and research tradition. These are shown in Figure 6.1. The first perspective is that of 'teaching effects', which encompasses sets of teaching behaviours or skills. Within this extensive literature, consistently high levels of correlation are demonstrated between student achievement scores and classroom processes. The second perspective concerns the acquisition of a repertoire of 'models of teaching', which refers to distinct teaching approaches. The third perspective

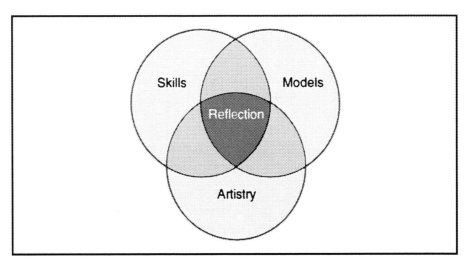

Figure 6.1 Three ways of thinking about teaching

is that of 'artistry', where teaching is seen as being a highly creative activity involving the use of sophisticated repertoires of responses and the ability to reflect upon practice.

The research literature on effective teaching demonstrates that there is a reasonable degree of consensus about the generic features or skill components of effective teaching (e.g. Good and Brophy 1980). While there are inevitable differences of emphasis and detail between findings, the overall consistency across so many of these studies is unquestionable. The research studies delineate between three important dimensions of effective teaching skills. Firstly, teachers' knowledge about their subject, curriculum teaching methods, the influence on teaching and learning of other factors and knowledge about one's own teaching. Secondly, the thinking and decision-making which occurs before, during and after a lesson, concerning how best to achieve the educational outcomes intended. Thirdly, the action or the overt behaviour by teachers undertaken to foster pupil learning. Taking these three dimensions a stage further, it is suggested that teaching skills possess certain features:

- they are intended to achieve a particular goal
- they take into account the particular context
- they require precision and fine tuning
- they are performed smoothly
- they are acquired through training and practice.

(Harris 1996)

The question of *how best to teach* has been most typically formulated in terms of what teaching approach, or method, is best. Studies into teaching styles, conducted most notably by Bennett (1976), have exposed the difficulty of identifying 'effective' teaching styles. It would appear from the research findings that a mixture of approaches or styles suited to the learning context is preferable. However, it is clear that in practice particular teaching styles have come to be associated with particular subjects. This is most evident in the secondary sector, where single subject teaching is the norm. There are also many primary schools where change in learning opportunity is most often associated with a change in subject content.

This matching of teaching approach to subject can inhibit the range of learning outcomes facilitated by the teacher and in effect, disenfranchise those pupils whose 'learning styles' do not coincide with the dominant teaching approach. Within our work we have been able to look at the preferred learning styles of some groups of pupils. These studies reveal that within any teaching group, preferred learning styles vary between students and that, for any one student, preferred learning styles vary according to the subject content. Genuine entitlement therefore requires that there is a range of teaching approaches in use in each subject of the curriculum and not merely a change in method between, for example, maths and physical education.

Our IQEA research findings suggest that where the teacher employs a range of specific strategies and teaching models more students demonstrate high levels of involvement in and commitment to the goals of a lesson. Joyce and Showers (1991) have defined a series of models of teaching which are designed to bring about particular kinds of student learning. They suggest that teachers should be able to identify these models and to select the ones they need to master in order to increase their teaching competence and teaching effectiveness. This perspective defines teaching in terms of distinct approaches designed to bring about particular kinds of learning and to help pupils become more effective learners. Unlike the early research on teaching styles, models of teaching are not premised on matching certain teaching behaviour to student outcomes. In contrast, much of the work on teaching models underlines the need for teachers to adopt a wide repertoire of teaching approaches rather than favouring one particular teaching approach or style.

Joyce *et al.* (1997) argue that models of teaching are really models of learning. They suggest that as teachers assist students with the acquisition of information, ideas, skills and values, they are essentially helping them to become more effective learners. When these models and strategies are combined, they have even greater potential for improving pupil learning. As Hopkins *et al.* (1994) make clear, when teachers adopt this experimental approach to their teaching, they are essentially taking on an educational idea and testing it out in their classrooms. It is in this 'experimentation' sense, that the use of teaching models is advocated as a strategy for school improvement.

While effective learning can take place in the absence of effective teaching, optimum results are most likely to occur when there is a good match of the two. This match has been characterised as 'artistry' and has been identified as an approach to the study of teaching which is of a different order from both the models of teaching and teaching skills approach. Artistry incorporates the recognition that teaching is highly creative and a highly personal activity. At the core of the interface between artistry, teaching skills and teaching models lies reflection (see Figure 6.1).

We have for a number of years now worked alongside our project schools to identify the conditions which build the school's capacity to engage in school improvement activities. At the classroom level this would also seem to be equally as important for effective teaching. Those teachers who are most aware of their own practice, i.e. those who engage in self-review and reflection, also tend to be those teachers who have the most extensively developed *repertoires*. In summary, effective teachers possess highly developed *repertoires* of teaching skills and *teaching strategies*.

Activity 6.1: teaching skills

Context

From the literature it has been shown that very effective teachers possess a set of generic skills which underpin their work. Yet teachers rarely talk about or review these teaching skills with other teachers. Schools tend to be communities consisting of people with different teaching skills and abilities, yet most often these are not articulated or shared. All teachers should be encouraged to talk about teaching and in particular to discuss their various strengths and teaching capabilities.

Briefing

Aims

- To provide staff with an opportunity to identify and review their teaching skills.
- To look specifically at how the range of teaching skills might be extended and refined through collaboration.

Process

Following a general introduction on the interrelationship between skills, models and artistry using Figure 6.1, there are four steps in the activity. Step 1 involves individuals in generating a list of teaching skills which they possess and rating them 1 (low) to 5 (high) according to how far they feel competent in each skill. Step 2 involves reviewing the skills against a checklist of seven skill areas in order to identify skill areas which are underdeveloped. Step 3 involves sharing the individual analysis with a colleague to identify areas of mutual support and development. Step 4 involves repeating Step 3 but in a group context where the possibilities for mutual support and development are enhanced.

Step 1   Make a list of all the teaching skills you think you possess and rate them 1 to 5 (1 lowest and 5 highest) in terms of your ability in each skill. Then make a list of those skills you would like to acquire which you currently feel are underdeveloped within your teaching skill repertoire.

Teaching skills

The teaching skills I possess are:

The teaching skills I would like to acquire, or refine are:

© IQEA – *Creating the Conditions for Classroom Improvement*

Step 2   Using the list below, group your listed skills using the seven headings. Are there any of the seven skill areas which do not appear or are under-represented in your list?

Seven teaching skills

Organising skills – to sort out materials and sources of information.

Analysis skills – to break down complex sources of information.

Synthesis skills – to build ideas into arguments.

Presentational skills – to clarify complex information without harming its integrity.

Assessment skills – to judge the work of pupils so that appropriate feedback can be given.

Management skills – to coordinate the dynamics of individual learners, groups and classes.

Evaluative skills – to improve teaching continually.

Step 3

With a colleague compare your list and analysis. Make a note of those skills you share and those skills which you both gave opposite scores to (i.e. 1 and 5). Having looked at your differing strengths, devise a strategy for mutual sharing and support in one or two of the skill areas.

Teaching skills we share:

Teaching skills which we rated differently:

Possible steps for sharing and collaboration in skill development:

Step 4

Repeat Step 3 as a small group. Devise a group strategy for mutual support and future development.

Activity 6.2: teaching styles

Context

The possession of a variety of teaching styles is vital to effective classroom practice. Unless staff develop a range of styles, it will remain the case that pupils with certain learning style preferences will be regularly disenfranchised from the learning process.

Briefing

Aim

- To explore individual teaching styles and to explore opportunities for extending teaching styles through collaborative investigation and practice.

Process

The activity consists of five steps. Steps 1 and 2 are 'tuning in' sessions; they raise individual awareness concerning preferred teaching approaches or styles. Step 3 is a more active session; it aims to stimulate discussion and joint planning. Encourage colleagues to fully share their views on teaching approaches and to search for similarities and differences in their preferred teaching styles. Steps 4 and 5 should facilitate joint planning and ideally should produce lesson plans for departmental and whole-school sharing.

Step 1

List the range of learning opportunities, experiences and activities which you make available to pupils during a typical day's teaching.

Range of learning opportunities:

Range of experiences:

Range of activities:

Step 2   Looking at your list, ask yourself the following questions:

- Is this pattern very different, or similar for each day? Are there set ways of working you prefer?

- Does this list suggest that you have a preferred teaching approach or style?

- Complete the grid below, placing a cross where you think you currently are in terms of teaching style and another cross on the continuum for where you would like to be:

Traditional	Progressive
Formal	Informal
Didactic	Experiential
Passive	Active

Step 3   Share your completed grid with a colleague from the same department and consider what the similarities and differences between your preferred teaching styles are.

Step 4   • Share with a colleague a recent lesson which you feel best illustrates your preferred teaching style.

• With your colleague replan that lesson using a different teaching style.

Step 5   Jointly sketch out a lesson plan to co-teach, using the teaching approach each of you least prefers.

Activity 6.3: teaching models

Context

Central to any notion of effective teaching is the ability to identify and draw upon relevant models of teaching for different learning situations or circumstances. This is particularly important when planning sequences of lessons which require different learning outcomes of the students. It is important to recognise that models of teaching can accomplish a range of curriculum and learning goals, but can also increase students' powers as learners. As students master information and skills, the result of each learning experience is not only the content they learn, but the greater ability they acquire to approach future learning tasks and to create programmes of study for themselves. In this respect models of teaching are also models of learning.

Briefing

Aims

- To promote understanding of different models of teaching and their classroom features.
- To allow staff to diagnose the range of teaching models they currently use and to actively explore unfamiliar models with colleagues.

Process

This activity is divided into four steps. Steps 1 and 2 require individual reflection and note-making and can be carried out during, or in preparation for, an INSET session. The second stage (Step 3) involves teachers working with colleagues to develop a more sophisticated and shared view of models of teaching. The third stage (Step 4) involves forward planning for staff development and training needs to be shared in the plenary session.

© IQEA – *Creating the Conditions for Classroom Improvement*

Step 1   Below is a description of four models of teaching and learning (adapted from Joyce *et al.* 1997). Reflect on whether you use them, or elements of them, in your own teaching.

Inductive teaching

The inductive model of learning teaches students to collect information and examine it closely, and through classifying data to generate concepts and create hypotheses.

Mnemonics

As a model of learning, mnemonics allows students to master large amounts of information and to gain conscious control of their learning processes.

Synectics

As a model of learning, synectics teaches metaphonic activity and encourages students to generate new and creative ideas.

Simulations

The simulations model of learning allows students to experience situations that they cannot access directly and to generate and test hypotheses on topics that could not be explored otherwise.

Step 2   Rate them as 1 (used infrequently) to 5 (used frequently).

Step 3   With a colleague discuss your selection of the models currently used and those you are less familiar with in practice. In particular:

• Make a list of words associated with the model of teaching you are most familiar with, i.e. how you would articulate the model to others.

• Identify the learning goals best addressed by each of the models.

Step 4   Share the responses within a group and decide:

• What teaching models might colleagues like to explore further?

• Who has expertise in the area?

• How can we best organise ourselves as a staff to facilitate staff development and support?

• What range of models would we need to develop in our school in order to meet the learning needs of all our students?

Activity 6.4: reflection

Context

We have suggested that enquiry and reflection are important processes in school improvement and that teacher enquiry and reflection are equally important in classroom improvement. Indeed, a willingness to reflect upon one's teaching and to record these reflections in a systematic way is a feature of highly skilled practitioners. This activity focuses upon the process of reflection and provides a format for paired observation, that is, pairing of teachers who undertake to observe one another in a classroom setting and offer feedback.

Although Step 1 is not essential, we would recommend that it is undertaken as a preparatory activity, preferably on a whole-school or departmental basis. It is important to remember that this activity will probably take place over a number of weeks.

Briefing

Aims

- To underline the view that all teachers should reflect upon their teaching.
- To provide an opportunity for colleagues to share one another's classroom practice.

Process

This activity takes place in four separate steps. Step 1 is designed to raise colleagues' awareness of the importance of reflection. Step 2 introduces a protocol for paired observation. Step 3 provides the opportunity for reflection and sharing. Step 4 encourages discussion and further planning for paired observation.

Step 1   Think of one lesson you have recently taught that was successful. Briefly complete the following statements:

1. The features which made the lesson successful were . . .

2. I judged it as a good lesson because . . .

3. I think the students thought that the lesson was good because . . .

4. Next time I'll improve the lesson by . . .

Think of one lesson you have recently taught that was unsuccessful. Briefly complete the following statements:

1. The features which made the lesson unsuccessful were . . .

2. I judged it as an unsuscuse lesson because . . .

3. I think the students thought that the lesson was not successful because . . .

4. Next time I'll improve the lesson by . . .

Step 2

Paired observation involves teachers acting as a mirror to a colleague reflecting back to him or her their own classroom practice. When planning shared observation, the following stages may prove useful.

Select pairings

These need to reflect the purpose of observation and involve colleagues who are comfortable with one another.

Arrange a pre-observation planning meeting

At this meeting it is important to identify the focus of the observation, those aspects of classroom practice which need to be recorded to shed light on the focus (i.e. what do we count as evidence?) and how the information will be recorded.

Timetable the observation

The particular lesson to be observed needs to be agreed in advance and to reflect the focus.

Carry out post-observation feedback

This needs to take place as soon as possible after the observation. It should provide an opportunity for both partners to 'make sense' of the experience, and for the observer to help the teacher to consider what developments (if any) in practice he or she might target.

Reverse roles and repeat

Step 3

Using the proforma in Step 1, complete the most appropriate statement, i.e. was the lesson successful or unsuccessful. Then share your notes and reflections with each other.

Step 4

In pairs discuss:

- What have we learned from one another about the process of reflection?

- What have we learned about acting as an observer to a colleague?

- What questions need to be added to those already asked in order to make the reflection process more developmental?

CHAPTER 7

Pedagogic partnerships

Teacher development takes place most effectively in a school where there is a culture of collaboration. Working with a colleague not only dispels feelings of professional isolation, but also assists in enhancing practice. Our research suggests that teachers are better able to implement new ideas within the context of supportive collegial relationships. This feeling of being part of a professional group within the school is therefore an important classroom condition, which enables teachers to function effectively and continue to improve their teaching. Within the context of development work this is best achieved through:

7.1 teachers discussing with each other the nature of teaching strategies and their application to classroom practice and schemes of work;

7.2 establishing specifications or guidelines for the chosen teaching strategies;

7.3 agreeing on standards used to assess student progress as a result of employing a range of teaching methods;

7.4 mutual observation and partnership teaching in the classroom.

Overview

The recognition that teachers develop most effectively as part of a professional team, dedicated to the improvement of teaching and learning, has led to an international clarion call for the reculturing of schools along collaborative lines (Fullan 1994, OFSTED 1994, Hopkins *et al.* 1988). Hargreaves (1995:15) has characterised such an environment as a community of learners:

> Collaborative cultures turn individual learning into shared learning. Attending to structures so that they help people connect, and designing tasks so they increase our capacity and opportunities for learning, spreads such learning across the entire organisation.

In a supportive school environment there are usually the structures already in place to effect change and improvement. Joyce (1992) has distinguished, helpfully in our opinion, between the two key elements of staff development: the workshop and the workplace.

The *workshop*, which is equivalent to the best practice on the traditional INSET course, is where teachers gain *understanding*, see *demonstrations* of the teaching strategy they may wish to acquire, and have the opportunity to *practice* them in a non-threatening environment. If the intention is to transfer those skills from the workshop into the *workplace* – the classroom and school – then merely attending the workshop is insufficient. The research evidence is very clear that skill acquisition and the ability to transfer vertically to a range of situations requires 'on-the-job-support'. This implies changes to the workplace and the way in which staff development is organised in schools. In particular, this means the opportunity for *immediate and sustained practice, collaboration and peer coaching*, and *studying development and implementation*. It is very difficult to transfer teaching skills from INSET sessions to classroom settings without alterations to the school's workplace conditions. Successful schools pay careful attention to their workplace conditions.

We have not as yet built such a robust infrastructure for staff development within our schools. Such an infrastructure would involve portions of the school week being devoted to staff development activities such as curriculum development and implementation, new models of teaching, regular observation sessions and on-site coaching. Integral to these activities is a commitment to reviewing one's performance as a prelude to development. It is within this context that classroom research is a fundamental staff development activity.

The Joyce and Showers' (1995) work on staff development, in particular their peer coaching strategy, has in recent years transformed our thinking on staff development. It is here that there is the closest link with classroom research techniques, especially observation. Joyce and Showers identified a number of key training components which when used in combination have much greater power than when they are used alone. The major components of training are:

- presentation of theory or description of skill or strategy
- modelling or demonstration of skills or models of teaching
- practice in simulated and classroom settings
- structured and open-ended feedback (provision of information about performance)
- coaching for application (hands-on, in-classroom assistance with the transfer of skills and strategies to the classroom).

Based on this analysis, Joyce and Showers (1995) summarised the 'best knowledge' we have on staff development like this:

- the use of the integrated theory–demonstration–practice–feedback training programme to ensure skill development
- the use of considerable amounts of practice in simulated conditions to ensure fluid control of the new skills

- the employment of regular on-site coaching to facilitate vertical transfer
  – the development of new learning in the process of transfer
- the preparation of teachers who can provide one another with the needed coaching.

This condition of 'pedagogic partnerships' contributes to the establishing of this infrastructure by providing the opportunity for teachers to *talk about teaching*. School improvement strategies should as a consequence create the conditions whereby teachers can develop a discourse about, and language for, teaching. The activities which follow are, therefore, an attempt to bring together those aspects of *pedagogic partnership* which the IQEA Project schools have found most helpful in promoting classroom improvement.

Activity 7.1: teachers discussing with each other the nature of teaching strategies and their application to classroom practice

Context

Learning and teaching in the classroom predominantly take place through interpersonal communication between teachers and pupils. The context in which this communication occurs and the relationships between teachers and pupils are neither fixed nor predetermined. Rather they are constructed by the teacher and the pupils and negotiated by them as they act and react through verbal and non-verbal behaviour. Effective pupil learning depends largely upon strong and positive management of classroom communication in all its forms and situations. In turn, effective classroom teaching depends upon strategies to enhance effective communication.

Briefing

Aims

- To explore effective classroom strategies.
- To establish more enhanced opportunities for innovation in the classroom.

Process

The activity consists of four steps. Step 1 is a 'tuning in' session; it raises colleagues' awareness. Step 2 is an active session; it aims to stimulate discussion and problem-solving. Step 3 is a sharing activity which encourages colleagues to fully share their ideas and to search for similarities and differences amongst their proposals. Step 4 is not only a summarising stage; colleagues should also try to devise some action points for developing different strategies in their classroom.

Step 1   Think of a lesson you have recently taught, and list the strategies used
during that lesson to take account of pupils' views or ideas.

During the lesson the opportunities for pupils to share their ideas or
thoughts with me were as follows:

© IQEA – *Creating the Conditions for Classroom Improvement*

Step 2   Form into groups of three. Each group is asked to consider one of the situations and then to decide which strategies might be used in this situation. Ask each member of the group to keep their own notes of the plan they devise as a group.

Situations

1. There are one or two pupils in your class who never contribute to a class discussion and others who rarely listen to what other pupils say.

2. A new teacher has asked you for some advice on groupwork and in particular how to encourage pupils to listen to each other.

3. As a result of an inspection, a group of teachers are asked to review the use of talk in their classrooms. The inspectors had reported that this was an area of general weakness.

Step 3   When every group has completed Step 2, reform the groups in such a way that each new member of the group has a plan for a different situation. Each member now describes their situation, presents their plans and invites questions and discussion.

Step 4   Each group should now agree a summary of the key strategies that have emerged.

Activity 7.2: establishing specifications or guidelines for the chosen teaching strategies

Context

The effective implementation of teaching strategies depends upon the implicit and explicit understanding of what the strategy will look like in the classroom. Consequently, it is important for teachers to establish and share specifications for chosen teaching strategies.

Briefing

Aim

- To identify ways of generating specifications for teaching strategies.

Process

This activity will explore ways of generating specifications for different teaching strategies. Step 1 will involve teachers in diagnosing which teaching strategies they use most in their teaching. Step 2 will involve them in generating a specification for teacher and student action during the activity. Step 3 will focus on developing a student behaviour specification.

Step 1   Individually, complete the following teaching strategy self-assessment sheet by noting which strategies you use most frequently and less frequently in your teaching. Then with a colleague compare lists.

Teaching strategies	Used often	Used sometimes	Used never
Accuracy stressed			
Accurate recall			
Action planning			
Brainstorming			
Case study			
Choice of activities			
Classwork			
Clear goals expressed			
Comprehension			
Data collection			
Demonstrations			
Discussion			
Group interaction			
Groupwork organised			
'Gut' feelings asked for			
Handouts			
Investigations			
Lecture			
Mistakes allowed			
Note-taking			
Open-ended questions asked			
Paired work			
Planning of work by pupils			
Practising skills			
Problem-solving			
Reflection on experience			
Relevance of work explained			
Reporting back methods varied			
Role play			
Scientific experiments			
Simulations used			
Specialisms tapped			
Testing			
Thoroughness stressed			
Variety of approaches			
Video			
Working alone			
Worksheets			

Step 2   With a colleague, decide upon a strategy you use least often and try and complete the following grid, which itemises what is required for this activity to be effectively implemented.

Understanding of what is required

Of the teacher

• Introduction

• During the activity

• Following the activity

Of the students

• Introduction

• During the activity

• Following the activity

© IQEA – *Creating the Conditions for Classroom Improvement*

Step 3   Having specified what is required of the teacher and student now try and specify more exactly expected student behaviour, using the example below.

Student learning behaviour

Student preparation
Students attend with the required equipment, which is placed to hand on the desk in readiness. Topics are read about before they are taught.

Note-taking
Students are able to take notes from text, television and video. This they do without instruction from the teacher.

Active listening
Students listen attentively, making a note of questions for themselves and adding their own ideas.

Asking questions
Students ask relevant questions.

Answering questions
Students answer open-ended questions at length, mentioning real examples and giving details.

Activity 7.3: agreeing on ways of assessing student progress as a result of employing a range of teaching methods

Context

Developing and implementing a range of teaching methods requires some means of student assessment in order to judge the impact of the development. Consequently, it is important that prior to employing a range of teaching methods, ways of assessing student progress are agreed. This will ensure that teachers receive continual feedback concerning the relative effectiveness of the various strategies or models implemented.

Briefing

Aim

- To consider existing and new ways of assessing student progress as a result of employing different teaching methods.

Process

This activity involves teachers in discussing the ways they currently assess student progress and evaluating some potentially different ways of making this assessment. Step 1 involves teachers listing their current ways of assessing student progress and requires teachers to consider the limitations of existing assessment tools. Steps 2 and 3 involve teachers in considering different assessment techniques and deciding how they could be incorporated as a means of evaluating student progress resulting from different teaching methods.

Step 1	With a colleague from the same department, list the ways in which you currently assess pupil progress. Having made the list, decide which of these would be suitable to provide evidence of pupil progress from different teaching approaches. The questions which might help the group are:

- If we employed a different teaching method, which of these measures would be a good indicator of successful implementation?

- Do we need additional assessment tools?

- What kind of assessment might be most suited to eliciting information about pupil progress, as a result of different teaching models or approaches?

Then make a list of the current limitations of the existing assessment procedures for the explicit purposes of illuminating differences resulting from different teaching methods.

Step 2

Regroup into a cross-departmental group and share your lists. Do other departments have other ways of assessing pupil progress that might be suited to exploring the impact of different teaching models? Decide as a group which existing assessment mechanisms might be used across *all* departments for the purpose of exploring teaching models.

Step 3

As a cross-departmental group, consider the self-assessment sheet on the following page and decide how this might be used to record differences between different teaching models, or approaches, if completed before the implementation of a new approach by the teachers involved and then several months later.

Self-assessment sheet

Fill in your responses by circling a number. Score:

1 Never
2 Rarely
3 Sometimes
4 Always

Student and group attitudes, motivation and commitment

Most students are confident	1	2	3	4
Most students have positive attitudes to the subject	1	2	3	4
Most students have positive attitudes to learning	1	2	3	4
Most students work together	1	2	3	4
Most students are supportive of each other's learning	1	2	3	4
Most students have a strong commitment to achieving high grades	1	2	3	4
Achievement and success are celebrated	1	2	3	4
Student self-esteem is enhanced by the course	1	2	3	4
Most students receive regular positive feedback about their progress	1	2	3	4

Understanding of what is required

Most students understand intended learning outcomes of the course	1	2	3	4
Most students understand assessment criteria and standards required	1	2	3	4
Most students understand relevance of any activity to the course	1	2	3	4
Most students understand structure of the course and examination	1	2	3	4
Most students are able to make links between units of the course	1	2	3	4
Most students know their own abilities in relation to the course	1	2	3	4
Most students know their own learning targets and goals	1	2	3	4
Most students are committed to those goals and targets	1	2	3	4

Student learning behaviour

Most students prepare and plan for the learning activities	1	2	3	4
Most students organise their own learning	1	2	3	4
Students review their prior learning before commencing a topic	1	2	3	4
Most students collect information about future topics	1	2	3	4
Most students take part in discussions and question and answer sessions	1	2	3	4
Most students take notes from teacher expositions	1	2	3	4
Most students review their own progress	1	2	3	4

Opportunities for student responsibility

Open-ended questions are asked by the teacher	1	2	3	4
Open-ended tasks are provided by the teacher	1	2	3	4
Tasks are challenging but achievable	1	2	3	4
Tasks provide the space for students to come to their own solutions	1	2	3	4
Most students are able to learn from mistakes	1	2	3	4
Most students are regularly able to review their work with the teacher	1	2	3	4
Most students are able to identify their own learning goals	1	2	3	4

Activity 7.4: mutual observation and partnership teaching in the classroom

Context

How do teachers connect their lessons to what their pupils already know? How do we find ways of personalising learning? As with so many of the topics addressed in this book, it is impossible to provide definitive answers to these questions. Teaching is a complex, personal business, and individual practitioners seem to be able to make particular approaches work effectively in ways that others would find impossible.

Our experiences suggest, however, that one particular aspect of practice does seem to be essential to the task of making connections with the pupils' existing knowledge: that is the use of questions.

While a lot of research has been carried out in this area, it does not in itself provide clear-cut priorities for action. By and large it is argued that divergent questions are better than convergent questions that high-level or complex questions are better than lower-level or simple questions, and that 'thought' questions are better than 'fact' questions. Some research also suggests that the frequency of questions is related to learning outcomes, possibly because this tends to be associated with teaching styles that are well organised and purposeful, and because of the opportunities it provides for pupils to express themselves orally. There is also evidence suggesting that it is important to allow pupils sufficient time to think about their responses to questions.

Briefing

Aims

- To examine ways in which questioning is used during lessons.
- To explore the value of mutual observation as a means of stimulating development of practice.

Process

This activity has to be carried out over a period of weeks. In addition to the focus on questioning, it can illustrate the potential of classroom observation. Where this is new, it needs to be set up carefully. We have sometimes found it useful if one pair of staff members try it out on behalf of the whole staff, preferably with a senior colleague volunteering to be observed first.

Prior to the observations, an introductory meeting is held to set the agenda and plan the partnerships. Then, following a period when observations occur, another meeting is held to debrief the experiences. Throughout, it is important to emphasise the importance of the technical dialogue that the activity fosters.

Step 1

An initial meeting of staff is held to begin discussion of the role of questioning in lessons as a means of helping pupils to connect existing knowledge to new learning. The context-setting text above can be used to facilitate this. Towards the end of this meeting partnerships are formed that will be used for a process of mutual observation. Activity 6.4 provides detailed guidelines on the establishment of such partnerships. In summary, it proposes five stages as follows:

- select pairings

- arrange a pre-observation planning meeting

- timetable the observation

- carry out post-observation feedback

- reverse roles and repeat.

Step 2

- Partners plan and carry out observations based on the following overall format.

> **Effective questioning**
>
> Research suggests that although the effectiveness of a question depends on context, in general good questions tend to be:
>
> 1. *Clear*
> They describe precisely the specific points to which pupils are to respond.
>
> 2. *Brief*
> The longer the question the more difficult it is to understand.
>
> 3. *Natural*
> They are phrased in natural, simple language and adapted to the language level of the class.
>
> 4. *Purposeful*
> Purposeful questions help achieve the lesson's intents.
>
> 5. *Sequenced*
> This involves using earlier responses to formulate further relevant questions.

- In observing your colleague, look for, and keep, a record of examples of each of these.

Step 3

A further meeting is held at which each pair of teachers reports in general terms on what has emerged from their observations and discussions. This would be significantly enriched if some colleagues are prepared to allow extracts of video recordings of their lessons to be analysed.

CHAPTER 8

Reflection on teaching

We have observed that those teachers who recognise that enquiry and reflection are important processes in classroom improvement find it easier to sustain improvement effort around teaching and learning practices. Central to the conditions which promote the effective use of enquiry and reflection as developmental tools are:

8.1 systematic collection and use of classroom-based data in decision-making;

8.2 effective strategies for reviewing progress and impact of classroom innovation and development;

8.3 widespread involvement of colleagues in the process of data collection;

8.4 clear ground rules for the collection, control and use of school-based data.

Overview

We have for a number of years worked alongside our project schools to identify the management arrangements or 'conditions' which build the school's capacity to engage in school improvement activities. One of these conditions is a commitment to school-level enquiry and reflection (Hopkins *et al.* 1994, Hopkins and West 1994). Indeed, we have observed that those schools which recognise that enquiry and reflection are important processes in school improvement find it easier to sustain improvement effort around established priorities, and are better placed to monitor the extent to which policies actually deliver the intended outcomes for pupils, even in these times of enormous change. Ironically, we have found that information gathered by outsiders, be they inspectors or consultants, is often seen as having more significance than information which is routinely available to those within the school community. However, we have observed that where schools understand the potential of internally generated information about progress or difficulties, they are better placed to exploit opportunities and to overcome problems.

There is a long tradition of classroom-based action research providing data for the processes of reflection and evaluation of teaching. This research can be undertaken by skilled colleagues or external consultants (Good and Brophy 1980, Hopkins 1993), or indeed by what has been termed 'reflection-in-action', where the teacher's own observations and inferences are used (Altrichter and Posch 1989). Although teachers work alone, the processes of reflection, research and evaluation are most effective in school improvement where they constitute a group activity. Because these processes are grounded in the teacher's own 'craft-knowledge', the findings are less theoretical, more practical and more applicable to similar classroom contexts within the school.

A major area of focus within IQEA Project schools therefore, has been to encourage scrutiny of the current and potential use of school-generated data in school decision-making. Of course, in adopting this focus, we have been aware that it is sensible to try to work with questions that need to be answered, with methods that are feasible and that neither intrude on, nor disrupt, the school's patterns of activity. Within these parameters we have urged participating schools to adopt a systematic approach to information collection, analysis and interpretation, particularly where information about the *impact*, rather than the implementation, of improvement programmes is wanted. We have also encouraged schools to involve all staff in this information management process – the data routinely available to staff, and the 'sense' they make of it, is a potentially important aid to decision-making.

As the focus within the IQEA Project schools has shifted away from how the school is managed to a more explicit focus on classroom practice, we have seen that many teachers have taken what has become the habit of enquiry with them. Consequently, there appears to be a much more self-conscious and open commitment to enquire into and reflect on classroom processes and outcomes. We see this as a natural counterpart to the school-level enquiry processes which have already been established.

We also see evidence that this is a most powerful classroom 'condition', one which interacts with and enhances the impact of other key classroom conditions. Thus, teachers who are self-critical of their own practice as a matter of routine appear, in the IQEA schools at least, to be those teachers who have the most extensively developed repertoires, and also seem to be the teachers who are most aware of the many things that are happening in the classroom at any one time. There is also a close overlap between those teachers in the IQEA schools who engage in regular self-evaluation and those who engage in classroom-level curriculum development.

Parenthetically, research that we have been conducting elsewhere suggests that teacher perceptions of student achievement correlate highly with their perceptions of the effectiveness of the school in terms of *enquiry* and *reflection*, staff development, and collaborative planning (Hopkins and Terrell 1995).

Activity 8.1: systematic collection and use of classroom-based data in decision-making

Context

Why is classroom-based data useful? It seems from research that very successful teachers have a positive regard for their pupils and are able to demonstrate that in their classroom practice. Classrooms can be seen as small communities consisting of people with different points of view and expectations. The aim should be to encourage everybody to have a positive regard for each member of the class, teacher or pupil. The assumption is that the classroom will be more effective in achieving its goals when everybody feels involved in making decisions and committed to broadly the same purposes.

Briefing

Aims

- To provide staff with an opportunity to analyse their relationships with pupils using classroom-based data.
- To look specifically at how the relationships with pupils might be enhanced using classroom-based data.

Process

Following a general introduction to the topic, Step 1 involves individuals reflecting upon and making notes about their relationships with pupils. If there is time, it would be helpful to invite pairs of colleagues to compare their ideas before moving on to the next step. Step 2 focuses upon the use of potential development of a classroom observation schedule. Groups of four or five would be most appropriate here. It might be that different groups address different issues concerning classroom observation. Step 3 involves members of the groups in recording their analysis on the form that is provided. Finally, Step 4 widens the discussion to a consideration of overall school policy in light of the discussion and analysis. It might conclude with discussion of actions to be taken.

Step 1

Before we discuss the issue of relationships with pupils in detail, make some notes about the ways in which you demonstrate a positive regard for pupils in everyday teaching:

I show positive regard for pupils in lessons by:

Step 2

Divide into working groups. Each group has to decide upon one or two aspects of demonstrating a positive regard for pupils, for example:

- listening

- showing interest

- praise

- recognition

- concern

- attentiveness

and design an observation checklist for classroom observational purposes. This checklist should list those classroom behaviours that would be expected from the teacher who is demonstrating positive relationships with pupils.

**Checklist of teacher's classroom behaviour:
positive attitude towards pupils**

Step 3

As a group, consider the following questions with respect to the checklist you have developed. Make notes of your own views during the discussion.

How might this checklist be used?

Who would use it? When?

What could happen with the observation data collected?

Step 4

Present your findings to the other groups. Discuss the following questions:

- Could these checklists encourage a more positive regard for pupils?
- How might they be improved?
- What could the checklists suggest about current classroom practice?
- What have you learned from this exercise?

Activity 8.2: effective strategies for reviewing progress and impact of classroom innovation and development

Context

As people learn about, prepare for, use and refine new practices, they move through a series of stages which need to be reviewed at regular intervals. It has been shown that teachers move through various stages during an innovation or development. These stages have been characterised as a focus on self, task and impact. Initially, staff are concerned about their own situation and want to know how the innovation will impact upon them. Later on, when the innovation is implemented, there is much more chance of questions concerning the impact of the innovation upon teaching and learning.

Briefing

Aim

- To consider effective strategies for reviewing the impact of an innovation.

Process

This activity introduces three strategies for reviewing the progress of a classroom innovation or development. Step 1 involves self-diagnoses of the impact of an innovation at the school, teacher and pupil level. It then requires teachers to consider how the impact of an innovation might be enhanced and developed in a practical way. Step 2 focuses upon data collection methods and encourages teachers to evaluate the appropriateness of different methods. Step 3 engages teachers in the process of planning with each other some form of data collection and enquiry.

Step 1   Using the grid below, with a colleague think of a recent innovation and fill in your response in the right-hand column. On a scale of 1 to 10 rate your responses. Score 1 for 'not at all' and 10 for 'extensively'.

Impact level

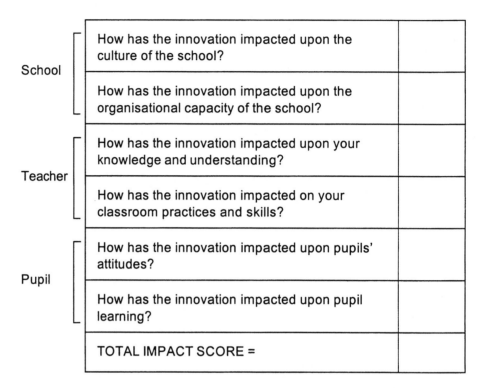

School	How has the innovation impacted upon the culture of the school?	
	How has the innovation impacted upon the organisational capacity of the school?	
Teacher	How has the innovation impacted upon your knowledge and understanding?	
	How has the innovation impacted on your classroom practices and skills?	
Pupil	How has the innovation impacted upon pupils' attitudes?	
	How has the innovation impacted upon pupil learning?	
	TOTAL IMPACT SCORE =	

Step 2   Share your grid with another pair. Have they reached similar conclusions about the scores given at each stage?

Step 3   As a group decide which level of impact is appropriate at the school, teacher and pupil level for the innovation in question. As a group brainstorm a range of strategies which could be used to raise the overall impact score. These should be recorded and shared with the other groups.

© IQEA – *Creating the Conditions for Classroom Improvement*

Activity 8.3: widespread involvement of colleagues in the process of data collection

Context

The amount of information available within schools is extensive but often teachers have little time to engage in the process of data collection. Yet this process is a potentially powerful means of reflection and development. One of the most positive ways in which staff can support each other is through collaborative data collection focused upon a particular issue. This data collection can serve several purposes. It can provide opportunities to share 'good practice' and learn from each other and can open up classrooms and stimulate a school-level debate about quality teaching and learning issues.

Briefing

Aim

- To consider ways of involving colleagues in the process of data collection.

Process

This activity involves three steps. Step 1 involves the teachers in an analysis of the strengths, weaknesses, opportunities and threats surrounding data collection and analysis with colleagues. Step 2 explores the various means of collecting data and requires participants to select those data collection tools which are most suited to collaborative data collection. Step 3 considers the stages of planning required for collaborative enquiry and reflection.

Step 1

With a colleague think about the strengths, weaknesses, opportunities and threats to the widespread involvement of colleagues in the process of data collection. Complete the grid below and consider the extent to which barriers can be overcome and weaknesses offset to gain the benefits and opportunities listed.

Involvement in data collection SWOT analysis grid

Strengths	Weaknesses	Opportunities	Threats

- How might threats be overcome?

- How might weaknesses be offset?

© IQEA – *Creating the Conditions for Classroom Improvement*

Step 2

In groups consider the following table of possible data collection methods and decide upon a potential focus or issue which would concern all teaching staff. Then decide which of these data collection methods could be used most effectively to collect data, on the issue in question, by a widespread group of colleagues.

Tool	Particular uses
Interview	To obtain information which would not be easily obtained from a questionnaire, e.g. sensitive, personal information
Audio tape recording	To obtain complete records and detailed evidence
Video tape	To obtain information which can be used later in a diagrammatic way. A complete visual record
Questionnaire	To obtain specific information and feedback from a potentially large number of people
Survey	Appropriate when large samples are involved
Observation	Appropriate for looking at teacher–pupil relationships or interaction in the classroom
Logs, diaries	For obtaining insight into pupils' views or ideas about an initiative

Step 3

Having decided a focus and a means of data collection, the next stage is to plan the data collection process with colleagues. In a group, consider the following questions, which will allow you to plan your data collection. If any one or more of the questions prove impossible to answer, it is probably best to reconsider your focus or data collection methods.

Planning data collection with colleagues

1. What is the focus of your joint enquiry/investigation?

2. What type of data collection tool is best suited to this focus? Why?

3. Who will design the data collection instrument?

4. Who will trial and test it?

5. When will the data collection take place? How do we ensure that everyone is involved in the data collection process?

6. Who will analyse the data?

7. How do we share the findings from the data analysis with each other and other colleagues?

© IQEA – *Creating the Conditions for Classroom Improvement*

Activity 8.4: clear ground rules for the collection, control and use of school-based data

Context

When collecting school-based data, it is important to establish shared protocols and ground rules concerning the collection, control and use of the data. If data is to be used in a developmental way, the procedures for data collection have to be agreed by those involved. This means that prior to the data collection period, a set of principles or ground rules needs to be devised and shared.

Briefing

Aims

- To consider the protocol issues surrounding the collection of school-based data.
- To develop a set of basic ground rules which can be used in the collection of school-based data.

Process

This activity involves participants in considering the issues of data collection design and implementation. There are three steps in this process. Step 1 requires participants to consider four examples of school-based data collection and to generate a list of potential difficulties arising from each situation. Step 2 focuses upon ways in which such difficulties might be offset. Step 3 requires participants to consider a draft protocol for data collection and to judge its suitability for each of the four situations they have considered.

Step 1

In small groups consider each of the four data situations and explore what, if any, potential difficulties might arise if the data was collected in an insensitive or inappropriate way.

1. A group of three colleagues, in the same department, have agreed to evaluate each other's teaching methods. Each teacher observes a lesson of one of the others, having agreed an observation schedule. They also ask a small sample of pupils in each of the observed lessons to complete a questionnaire.

2. The work experience organiser has been asked by the Senior Management team to evaluate work experience. The team wants to know if work experience is operating smoothly, if it is being managed efficiently, and its effect on the curriculum. Data is collected from pupils, teachers, employers and parents, by way of interviews and questionnaires. The information gathered ranges from preparation for work experience to integration in the curriculum. Most of the school staff are involved in some way, e.g. visiting pupils during their placements.

3. The Personal and Social Education (PSE) team in a school agrees to evaluate its work and appoint one of its members to carry out the evaluation. Staff and pupils are interviewed about the current arrangements and future plans. A sample of students completes a questionnaire designed to record its level of satisfaction with the course.

4. The Senior Management team wishes to know the precise requirements for INSET by teachers who need some training in the use of technology equipment. A teacher is appointed to gather this information through a survey of all the staff, by the use of a questionnaire.

Step 2

As a group, discuss what types of preliminary consultation or briefing might be needed to ensure that the data collection process was viewed positively and was widely supported.

Step 3   Consider the following protocol for data collection. How suitable is this as a general set of principles? As a group, decide whether other principles are necessary to meet the needs of the four examples you have considered. Generate a final list and share with other colleagues.

Data collection protocol

- Information about the purposes of the data collection process should be shared.

- Involvement of colleagues is necessary.

- All implicated parties should be consulted.

- All implicated parties are updated as the data collection process moves into analysis and findings.

- The data collection should be diplomatic and non-threatening.

- There should be confidentiality assurances for those providing data.

- The outcomes and implications of the data collection process should be known, if possible, in advance.

CHAPTER 9

The journey of classroom improvement

A framework for classroom improvement

Throughout this book we have been attempting to establish a framework for classroom improvement that builds explicitly on enhancing the learning experiences, achievement and progress of pupils through working on the conditions existing within the classroom. This may be a somewhat different orientation to that of the school improvement centres that have recently burgeoned in this country. Many of them seem to focus on process or staff development activities rather than on creating learning environments that enhance the achievement of pupils. Our own definition of school improvement is therefore probably more precise and focused than that commonly used by many in this country at the moment. In our view, school improvement is about raising student achievement through focusing on the teaching/ earning process and the conditions which support it (Hopkins *et al.* 1994:3). One way of expressing this argument in the context of school improvement is found in Figure 9.1 (Hopkins 1997).

The centre of the series of concentric rings is powerful learning – the achievement and progress of students. The next ring comprises the essential ingredients of powerful teaching – the mix of teaching strategy, curriculum content and the learning needs of students. Powerful learning and powerful teaching are found in powerful schools, that is, schools that have organisational conditions supportive of high levels of teaching and learning. Some of the key elements of these conditions are found in the next ring – collaborative planning that focuses on student outcomes, staff development that is committed to the improvement of classroom practice, regular enquiry and reflection on the progress of students and the evolution of classroom practice, and the involvement of pupils and the community in learning. All of this activity takes place within, of course, the context of the national reform agenda – the outer ring. When all the rings are pulling in the same direction, then powerful learning is likely to be the result. All need to exist in a reciprocal relationship if student achievement is to be enhanced.

Successful school improvement

One way of understanding the relationship between the conditions and enhanced levels of student learning and achievement is to consider Joyce's analysis of the characteristics of effective large-scale school improvement initiatives (Joyce *et al.* 1993:72). These characteristics have tended to:

106

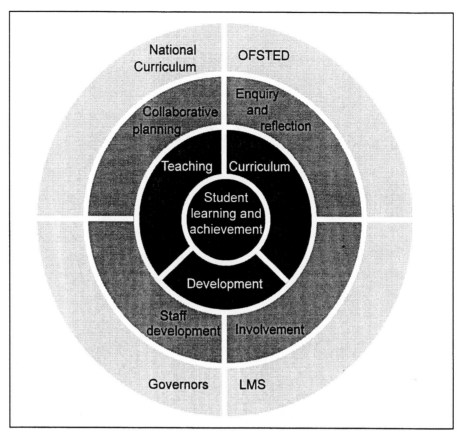

Figure 9.1 The circles of school improvement

- focus on specific outcomes which can be related to student learning, rather than adopt laudable but non-specific goals such as 'improve exam results'
- draw on theory, research into practice and the teachers' own experience in formulating strategies, so that a rationale for the required changes is established in the minds of those expected to bring them about
- target staff development, since it is unlikely that developments in student learning will occur without developments in teachers' practice
- monitor the impact of policy on practice early and regularly, rather than rely on 'post-hoc' evaluation.

These characteristics are highly consistent with the IQEA framework for school improvement. They illustrate how powerful learning (the first point), is contingent on powerful teaching (the second point), which is set within the context of the organisational conditions of the powerful school (the final two points). This interrelationship is a vital component of sustainable classroom improvement efforts.

We often use the metaphor of 'the journey' to describe our work within the classrooms of the schools involved in the IQEA Project. The image of the journey captures well the non-prescriptive and investigative nature of our collaboration.

So what does the journey of school improvement look like in practice? There are many faces to success, and we have noted some patterns and trends which we believe can apply to other schools and other systems. Although the metaphor of the journey implies an organic process, there do appear to be a number of distinct phases that teachers go through during school improvement work.

As we noted in our companion volume (Ainscow *et al.* 1994), schools will need to address the fundamental questions of:

- **Where are we now?**
- **Where do we want to be?**
- **What do we need to do?**
- **Where will we go next?**

The nature of the work implied by each of these will obviously vary from classroom to classroom. At times phases may co-exist, or be entered in an order different from the somewhat linear description we give below. But despite this we know of no teachers or schools which have been successful in their development work that have not, at some time or the other, worked within each of these phases.

A starting point – where are we now?

The major theme of this book is the creation of the internal conditions to support change. It is therefore helpful to take this as a key starting point – to ask the question 'where are we now?' We encourage teachers to review their classroom conditions early on in their school improvement journeys. Sometimes it is necessary to concentrate much more in the initial stages on improving the conditions in the classroom and limit work on the priorities. Activities designed to assess the internal conditions of the classroom can also be used to generate awareness and build commitment towards development work. The building of 'ownership' and making everyone aware of, if not involved in, school improvement is a vital early task.

Early in the IQEA Project we designed a rating scale to assist teachers to *review their internal conditions* at the level of the school. The scale also helps to establish a common language within the school to discuss development strategies. The early feedback from teachers convinced us that some (relatively straightforward) instrument which could help them diagnose the internal conditions of their school was useful. Using a similar logic we have devised for this book a rating scale to diagnose the conditions for classroom improvement.

The scale is based on the six conditions for classroom improvement described in previous chapters. There are four items for each condition drawn on the key ideas described in each of the conditions chapters; this gives 24 items in all. A version of the scale (which is photocopiable and copyright-free) is found in the Appendix. Although a computer program is available (from the authors on a Macintosh disk), the scale can be quickly and easily analysed by hand.

The scale, besides assisting in responding to the question 'where are we now?' can also be used to help *build commitment towards development work*. It gives a picture of the conditions for development within a classroom, and generates an interest among teachers for improvement activities. It also lays a strong foundation for the next phase: deciding where the teacher wants to be.

To illuminate this process in action we have chosen examples from six schools with whom we are currently working, as illustrations of the way in which classroom-based development has taken place in practice. Each of the schools selected one of the classroom conditions to focus upon in their developmental work. We begin each case study with the question 'where do we want to be?' on the assumption that each of these schools have used either the rating scale or a whole-school discussion to determine 'where are we now?'

Case study 1: authentic relationships

Where do we want to be?

This school identified the quality of teaching and learning as the main priority within the 1994–95 School Development Plan. Supported by the IQEA cadre group within the school, each department was invited to select its own classroom focus for development. Two departments (Technology and Science) decided to look at the quality of pupil–teacher interactions within their subject area.

What do we need to do?

Both departments selected Year 9 as the target for enquiry, and after discussion within the departments it was agreed that both would look at pupil–teacher interaction, using an observation schedule derived from the work of Marzano *et al.* (1992). The schedule was designed to investigate the extent to which teacher comments and behaviours contributed to the quality of classroom climate and relationships. Specifically, teacher actions which:

- increased pupils' sense of acceptance
- increased pupils' sense of comfort and order
- helped pupils to see the value of tasks and activities
- helped pupils understand what was expected of them in terms of tasks and activities

were logged, using a schedule which identified 20 different teacher actions/ behaviours. The observations were carried out by a member of the IQEA team.

There was slight variation between the two subject areas, but in both cases approximately two-thirds of teacher behaviours related to administrative or disciplinary matters, and only one-third to behaviours which were likely to create greater authenticity in the relationships between teacher and pupil. This 'balance' may of course be typical, certainly it compares with other studies which have looked at positive and negative feedback to pupils (e.g. Wheldall and Merrett 1989).

Where will we go next?

The investigations were not carried out in order to see whether practice was satisfactory or not, but to establish what practice was. Now there is a baseline against which changes can be measured, as the two departments embark upon a range of measures aimed at increasing the quality of pupil–

teacher interactions over time. There is also a clearer appreciation of the need to *work at* the development of appropriate classroom relationships, rather than assuming that this is something which teachers can establish intuitively.

Case study 2: boundaries and expectations

Where do we want to be?

One of the IQEA Project schools (a 14–19 Upper School) had been concerned for some time about the standards of pupil behaviour around the school. This growing unease was further increased by a 'ghost inspection' by the LEA, using the OFSTED framework and criteria. The report from this exercise suggested that in some subjects/classrooms pupil behaviour had deteriorated to the point where it was interfering with the quality of learning and, in some cases, inhibiting the range of teaching approaches being used.

What do we need to do?

One consequence of this was the identification of classroom behaviour management as a major school improvement focus, and a task group was established to carry forward the school's thinking and develop a strategy. A behaviour management policy and code of behaviour emerged from this task group's deliberations. These had wide-ranging implications for the reward and discipline systems in the school. However, one aspect of the action plan can be separated out. The school describes this as the 'lesson template' (see Figure 9.2).

As can be seen, the template is simply a checklist of 'dos and don'ts' for teachers – nothing on the list is at all profound or intellectually complex. But its value lies in the fact that it has been drawn up, that all members of staff have knowledge of it and that it directly addresses both the behaviours which were causing distractions and the *sources* of those behaviours (as they emerged from the task group's investigations). Consequently, the template offers the possibility of concerted, collective action across the school, which confronts the behaviour problem and offers each teacher the reassurance of not having to act alone.

Where will we go next?

Of course, the following of the template by teachers will not of itself resolve the difficulties which led the school to focus on this issue, but as a part of a wider revision of the school's discipline and reward policies, it has a role to play. Our feeling is that there are many teachers, even in relatively effective and well-regulated schools, who would welcome the systematic adoption of such an approach. There is no doubt that the struggle to maintain order on a lesson-by-lesson basis detracts from the quality of teaching and learning in many schools. Even if a secure classroom environment does not in itself actively promote school improvement, at a minimum it seems to be a prerequisite for the application of other improvement strategies.

Lesson template

1. *Pre-lesson*

   - Lesson plans must be prepared referring to aims and objectives, timings and attainment targets and levels.

   - Resources must be prepared and be appropriate to need.

   - The room layout must be considered in relation to objectives.

   - The subject matter must be understood.

   - Liaison with support staff, if appropriate, should occur.

2. *Entrance*

   - Students should come in quietly, sit down, remove coats and bags.

   - Attention must be secured (registration is one way of doing this).

3. *Beginning*

   In outlining the lesson, make clear:

   - its objectives and purposes

   - its content – as related to previous lesson(s)

   - its timing and pace in terms of tasks set

   - the assessment strategies to be used.

4. *Implementation*

   Teachers should demonstrate the following key features:

   - Teaching should be purposeful

     – planning and objectives should be clear and time should not be wasted.

   - Teaching should create and sustain interest:

     – content should be introduced with skill and imagination

     – pupils' interest should be maintained using a range of strategies.

© IQEA

Figure 9.2

Case study 3: planning for teaching

Where do we want to be?

The English Department in one IQEA school chose, as its focus for development, the use of differentiation in catering for different learning styles and differing abilities of pupils. The original intention was to adapt existing schemes of work within the department so that each would incorporate tasks suited to pupils within each learning style.

What do we need to do?

The typology used was one based upon Kolb's fourfold model (Kolb 1984). Various constraints led the departmental team to refocus, and concentrate upon producing a document on differentiation which could be used to inform the planning of all new schemes of work as well as the adaptation of existing ones. Team members were paired for the purposes of observation, and a schedule of questions for the teacher and of the observation foci in the lesson was drawn up. Teachers were asked about the scheme of work being used in the lesson, their confidence in it, the objectives of the lesson and any reasons for pupil groupings. The observation prompts related to identifying instances of differentiation by task and outcome, the setting of targets and the nature of teacher interventions. The impact of any variety in teaching approach on the lesson format was also noted.

The completed document defined differentiation and presented a series of strategies which could be used in the classroom to achieve it. The document stressed the importance of:

- diagnostic assessment of where pupils were in terms of their learning
- personalised as well as group targets, which should be negotiated with pupils
- the provision of a range of opportunities for learning
- thoughtful grouping of pupils
- skilled teacher interventions
- adapted materials
- a variety of sources of feedback for pupils.

Examples of subject-specific individual and group tasks were also given.

Where will we go next?

The document was used in the English Department to review and evaluate both the teaching methods used and the suitability of the content of its various schemes of work to cater for different abilities and learning styles. Because there were sections in the document which were relevant to any subject teacher, various departments within the school used it as a starting point for discussion and refinement of their own schemes. The document was also widely networked across the IQEA schools.

Case study 4: teaching repertoire

Where do we want to be?

Another IQEA school has taken teaching strategies as its focus over the last school year. The school was keen to involve all curriculum areas in the scrutiny of current teaching approaches and to encourage each curriculum group to experiment with at least one new approach, which could be monitored and evaluated. This experimentation took place in the context of a wider enquiry into the range of learning opportunities currently on offer, a review of existing approaches and expertise among the staff group, and an enquiry into the pupils' views on, and responses to, the variety of teaching approaches they encountered within the school.

What do we need to do?

In all, nine curriculum groupings responded to the invitation to participate, though inevitably some made better progress than others, particularly with regard to the development of teaching strategies. Nevertheless a range of 'new' approaches were experimented with – Creative Arts, for example, decided to look at the possibilities of synectics (see Joyce and Weil 1996), Modern Languages to adopt target language teaching within key curriculum 'pockets', Physical Education to explore the potential of video equipment in the development of pupils' performance skills.

One of the more sustained efforts to explore the range of learning opportunities on offer and to evaluate their effectiveness was undertaken by the Science Department. This department has been working with the IQEA Project within the school for the past four years, and has already undertaken a number of curriculum review and development projects. However, to date, these projects had tended to focus on curriculum content and assessment issues. Encouraged to explore the repertoire of learning opportunities available within science lessons, the department decided to look at these in conjunction with levels of pupil response or motivation in the particular learning situation. Having worked systematically through a process of self-review, to identify factors in lessons which seemed to be associated closely with levels of pupil motivation, colleagues in the department then moved into a period of deliberate 'experimentation'. This involved parallel observation of pupils using an observation schedule drawn up by the members of the department.

In the next phase of the enquiry colleagues shared findings from the observation programme and considered the implications. Although the findings suggested that levels of pupil motivation were not always satisfactory, it was the issues arising which interested the teachers most. For example, they felt that they were beginning to see tangible links between teaching approach and pupil response that could help with lesson planning. Colleagues were also becoming used to watching one another teach, and as a result found themselves talking much more about the impact of teaching approach on learning outcome. They were also learning that the design of an observation schedule was a complex business which needed to be approached in context – but that much could be learned from one another with more judicious analysis of one another's practice.

Where will we go next?

As a consequence, there has been a high level of commitment to carrying the observation programme forward into the next school year. The observation programme will be used to address a number of issues, including:

- recording and promoting as wide a range of lesson strategies as is feasible

- analysing in detail the factors which influence pupil motivation in laboratory-based lessons
- seeking opportunities for a wider use of reading and other tasks for which pupils can take much greater responsibility, reducing dependence on teachers for constant direction
- taking a closer look at how differentiation is practised in the classroom and its effects on pupils' motivation.

The department also hopes to promote the increased involvement of parents in contributing to a wider 'science curriculum' which supports work in school by encouragement and recognition of the learning opportunities available in the home. In this sense the notion of repertoire has been extended beyond the classroom and the school, to embrace and reinforce learning opportunities wherever they arise.

Science staff, like the other teachers in this school, have created a daunting agenda for themselves. However, this initial review of teaching approaches has certainly led to an increased commitment to develop both the variety of strategies available to teachers and the teachers' understanding of the factors to consider when selecting a particular approach.

Case study 5: pedagogic partnerships

Where do we want to be?

The Acting Head of a small rural primary school wanted to introduce the process of whole-school evaluation to her staff of six teachers in stages. She started by asking each of them to fill in a self-evaluation questionnaire during the summer vacation, which would identify areas of expertise as well as ones in which staff would welcome help, guidance and support. Staff reported their responses verbally at the first staff meeting of the autumn term. Using the questionnaires the Head negotiated with her staff a number of possible areas of enquiry, and suggested three pairings to pursue them.

What do we need to do?

A newly qualified teacher of Years 5 and 6 was paired with the Reception teacher to look at the effective use of IT in the classroom. The two Infants teachers chose two areas, differentiation in English and time management in the classroom. The two teachers of Years 3 and 4 also chose time management. Using the help of an external consultant, each pair agreed on the classroom focus for each enquiry, as well as the methodology to be used to collect data. There was also some discussion about the possible implications of each enquiry, for example for teacher planning, classroom organisation, teaching styles and the management of ancillary staff.

The Head then timetabled non-contact time for each of the staff to have a 'trial run' at observation, as well as up to a further two hours to undertake the actual observation of their partner's class. Staff used a mixture of domestically and commercially produced observation schedules. One teacher devised her own schedule to interview pupils on how they chose books from the class library.

After the collection of the data, staff again met with the external consultant to discuss appropriate forms of presentation. Each partner produced a separate report of their observations, and these were presented to a staff meeting in November.

Where will we go next?

The findings threw up some surprises: the teachers of Years 3 and 4, for example, had no idea that they asked so many questions in the course of a lesson. Even where there were few surprises, teachers felt that the practice that had been reviewed was now based upon hard evidence rather than their own hunches. One teacher said that she was now more confident in justifying to parents the nature of the reading material she provided in the classroom.

The findings also gave rise to staff discussions about effective classroom practice, for example, about the importance of the quality of support activities not directed by the teacher, and about the nature of teacher intervention in pupils learning about IT. The interest in the volume of questioning in Years 3 and 4 has given rise to one about the nature and quality of teachers' questions, and this has been agreed as a whole-school focus for the spring term.

Case study 6: reflection on teaching

Where do we want to be?

One of the IQEA schools has over the past year been researching the quality of learning opportunities and outcomes. This exercise was planned in three phases. In the *first phase*, teachers in the participating subject departments (eight in all) formed 'Research Groups'. These groups then planned classroom-level enquiries focusing on the quality of learning. Although each department selected its own points of focus, in each case there was a commitment to pursue this focus within a range of classrooms, and to pool the outcomes at a departmental level.

What do we need to do?

This sharing of experiences and reflections on the quality of learning itself raised a number of issues about teaching approach and classroom organisation, and there was a commitment to identify and to replicate the best practices across the department. In the *second phase* departmental research groups exchanged experiences and findings, with a view to identifying issues of whole-school interest and areas for whole-school development. In the *final phase* these were followed up and a deliberate strategy to disseminate practice implemented (supported where necessary by appropriate training).

Already much has emerged from this collaborative exercise in classroom-level enquiry. The Technology Department, for example, has looked at how colleagues use homework within the context of their teaching, and also at the response of pupils to the way homework is used. This revealed significant differences in practice between teachers. It also indicated that for many pupils some of the homework set, rather than being a tool for learning, actually reduced interest in and commitment to the subject. The department is revising its policy in light of the findings, and it is clear that this investigation will have implications for other departments.

Perhaps the most interesting enquiry has been carried out by the Humanities Research Group, where some staff have been looking into the significance of room layout and seating arrangements for learning. In this enquiry, a variety of seating arrangements were studied, using observation and interview programmes with pupils and teachers. The exercise increased in scope as it progressed, and produced some extremely interesting teacher and pupil perspectives, as well as a range of findings which have relevance for the practice of all teachers in the school (see Sharnbrook Upper School 1995).

Where will we go next?

Each departmental Research Group felt that it had produced something of value for their colleagues which could benefit the pupils in that department. Many have identified issues which will need further enquiry or have wider implications, but there is a clear sense of empowerment amongst those who have been involved. It seems that if the confidence to take a critical and self-critical look at classroom practice can be established, then classroom-level enquiry and reflection can do much to increase the quality of learning.

Journeying on

The nature of our research and development work within the IQEA Project is inevitably iterative. We engage in research and theory building by reviewing the knowledge base, gathering data, reflecting on outcomes, formulating hypotheses, testing them out and refining them – all in collaboration with schools in the network. So although our research into the 'classroom conditions' aspects of school improvement has completed its first stage of development, it is in the nature of our work that the conditions will still continue to be subject to further refinement.

One of our major concerns is to explicate how the focus on the internal conditions of the school contributes to an emerging theory of school development. The next major step in this process is to attempt to find some relationship between the school-level, the classroom-level and the student-level conditions. One such speculation is given below.

Table 9.1 Linking management factors to school improvement conditions

Key functions of management	School-level conditions	Classroom-level conditions	Pupil-level conditions
Motivation	Leadership	Authentic relationships	Orientation to learning
Control	Coordination	Boundaries and expectations	Adjustment to school
Direction / focus	Collaborative planning	Planning for teaching	Independent learning
Personal growth	Staff development	Teaching repertoire	Learning repertoire
Inclusiveness	Involvement	Pedagogic partnerships	Affinity to teacher
Monitoring impact	Enquiry and reflection	Reflection on teaching	Self-assessment

We hope that our continued work with schools will enable us to explore the interrelationship between the school, classroom and student level. We are already working with our schools towards a further book that focuses on the student-level conditions for school improvement conditions even more closely. In so doing, it is anticipated that we will be able to refine our conceptual, methodological and strategic understanding of school improvement even further.

Our continuing aim is not only to improve the quality of education for all our pupils, but to know how we do it, and through knowing, to refine our practice. We have already described our commitment to school improvement by using the metaphor of the journey. As we noted then, the quest for enhancing the quality of learning for all students knows no end – in concert with our schools, we simply journey on.

CHAPTER 10

An invitation . . .

As we have worked with schools during this period, we remain convinced that they need to adopt a more thorough and deep approach to change, one which takes account of the conditions necessary for school and classroom improvement. We hope that this book will serve to encourage teachers and schools to be relentless in pursuing improved teaching and learning for all pupils. Furthermore, we hope it will encourage teachers to actively create and sustain the conditions for improvement within their own classrooms.

We have tried in this book to present, in a practical and accessible way, some of what we have learned about school and classroom improvement over the past decade. We hope that teachers will find our advice realistic and the staff development activities challenging and helpful. We would therefore welcome any views about this book and the ideas it contains. This will allow us to refine our models of school and classroom improvement even further.

We look forward to hearing from you.

The classroom conditions rating scale

Following is a series of 24 statements about teacher practice in classrooms. We would like to know how far these statements match *your own* perception of teacher practice in your school, in other words, your *personal view* of it. There are no 'right' answers, we are seeking your opinion.

Please indicate your present post:

Support staff	
Teacher	
Management team	

and subject/teaching area _____

(The rating scale and analysis advice are adapted from *Mapping Change in Schools: The Cambridge Manual of Research Techniques*, Cambridge University (1994).)

Authentic relationships			
1.1	Teachers demonstrate positive regard for all pupils.		
	RARELY	SOMETIMES	OFTEN	NEARLY ALWAYS
1.2	Teachers conduct their relationships in the classroom in ways that demonstrate consistency and fairness and build trust.		
	RARELY	SOMETIMES	OFTEN	NEARLY ALWAYS
1.3	Teachers understand and show that communication with pupils involves listening as much as speaking.		
	RARELY	SOMETIMES	OFTEN	NEARLY ALWAYS
1.4	Teachers make their classrooms places where pupils can safely experiment with behaviours involving choice, risk-taking and personal responsibility.		
	RARELY	SOMETIMES	OFTEN	NEARLY ALWAYS

Boundaries and expectations			
2.1	Teachers establish clear boundaries to, and expectations of, pupil behaviour.		
	RARELY	SOMETIMES	OFTEN	NEARLY ALWAYS
2.2	Teachers promote a system of rewards and sanctions that emphasises expectations and promotes pupil self-esteem and self-discipline.		
	RARELY	SOMETIMES	OFTEN	NEARLY ALWAYS
2.3	Teachers use active management strategies to create and maintain an appropriate classroom environment.		
	RARELY	SOMETIMES	OFTEN	NEARLY ALWAYS
2.4	Teachers show consistency, without inflexibility, in responding to pupils and events.		
	RARELY	SOMETIMES	OFTEN	NEARLY ALWAYS

Planning for teaching			
3.1	Teachers build variety into lesson plans.		
	RARELY	SOMETIMES	OFTEN	NEARLY ALWAYS
3.2	Teachers adjust classroom arrangements in response to pupil feedback during lessons.		
	RARELY	SOMETIMES	OFTEN	NEARLY ALWAYS
3.3	Teachers employ strategies that enable pupils to find meaning in lesson activities.		
	RARELY	SOMETIMES	OFTEN	NEARLY ALWAYS
3.4	Teachers use homework to reinforce and extend learning.		
	RARELY	SOMETIMES	OFTEN	NEARLY ALWAYS

Teaching repertoire				
4.1	Teachers demonstrate a range of classroom management skills in the lessons.			
	RARELY	SOMETIMES	OFTEN	NEARLY ALWAYS
4.2	Teachers employ various teaching strategies or models within their lessons.			
	RARELY	SOMETIMES	OFTEN	NEARLY ALWAYS
4.3	Teachers trial and refine new teaching models as part of their own professional development.			
	RARELY	SOMETIMES	OFTEN	NEARLY ALWAYS
4.4	Teachers reflect on their classroom practice.			
	RARELY	SOMETIMES	OFTEN	NEARLY ALWAYS

Pedagogic partnerships				
5.1	Teachers discuss with each other the nature of teaching strategies and their application to classroom practice and schemes of work.			
	RARELY	SOMETIMES	OFTEN	NEARLY ALWAYS
5.2	Teachers establish specifications or guidelines for new teaching strategies.			
	RARELY	SOMETIMES	OFTEN	NEARLY ALWAYS
5.3	Teachers agree on standards used to assess student progress as a result of employing a range of teaching methods.			
	RARELY	SOMETIMES	OFTEN	NEARLY ALWAYS
5.4	Teachers engage in mutual observation and partnership teaching during lessons.			
	RARELY	SOMETIMES	OFTEN	NEARLY ALWAYS

Reflection on teaching				
6.1	Teachers use systematically collected classroom-based data in their decision-making.			
	RARELY	SOMETIMES	OFTEN	NEARLY ALWAYS
6.2	Teachers employ effective strategies for reviewing progress and the impact of classroom innovation on pupil progress.			
	RARELY	SOMETIMES	OFTEN	NEARLY ALWAYS
6.3	Teachers are widely involved in the process of data collection.			
	RARELY	SOMETIMES	OFTEN	NEARLY ALWAYS
6.4	Teachers establish clear ground rules for the collection, control and use of school-based data.			
	RARELY	SOMETIMES	OFTEN	NEARLY ALWAYS

Analysis

As the scale is primarily concerned with assessing and diagnosing a school's classroom conditions the analysis is best undertaken on an institutional rather than an individual basis. Similarly the analysis needs to be by sub-scale rather than item. A score of 1–4 is given to the 'rarely' (1), 'sometimes' (2), 'often' (3), or 'nearly always' (4) response for each item, and these are then totalled for each sub-scale, using the summary sheet below. The data make most sense if they are expressed as percentages. When the data are presented in this way it is easy to highlight patterns of responses, particularly when the percentage response for 'often' and 'nearly always' are added together. As the scale currently requests differentiation between 'management team', 'teacher' and 'support staff', and subject/teaching area, analyses can be done across sub-scales for these four groupings.

Summary sheet

	Rarely	Sometimes	Often	Nearly always
Authentic relationships				
Boundaries and expectations				
Planning for teaching				
Teaching repertoire				
Pedagogic partnerships				
Reflection on teaching				

References and
further reading

Ainscow, M., Hopkins, D., Southworth, G. and West, M. (1994) *Creating the Conditions for School Improvement*. London: David Fulton Publishers.

Ainscow, M., Hargreaves, D. H., Hopkins, D. (1995) 'Mapping the process of change in schools', *Evaluation and Research in Education* **9** (2), 75–90.

Altrichter, H. and Posch, P. (1989) 'Does the "grounded theory" approach offer a guiding paradigm for teacher research?' *Cambridge Journal of Education* **19** (1), 21–31.

Bennett, N. (1976) *Teaching Styles and Pupil Progress*. London: Pergamon Press.

Beresford, J. (1995a) 'Classroom conditions for school improvement: a literature review'. Prepared for International Congress for School Effectiveness and Improvement (ICSEI) Conference, London, October 1995. University of Cambridge Institute of Education mimeo.

Beresford, J. (1995b) 'The classroom conditions scale'. University of Cambridge Institute of Education mimeo.

Brandes, D. and Ginnis, P. (1990) *The Student-Centred School: Ideas for Practical Visionaries*. Oxford: Blackwell.

Brown, S., Duffield, J., Riddell, S. (1995) 'School effectiveness research: the policy makers' tool for school improvement', *EEAR Bulletin*, March.

Buber, M. (1970) *I and Thou*. New York: Charles Scribner's Sons.

Cambridge University (1994) *Mapping Change in Schools*. Cambridge: University of Cambridge Institute of Education.

Creemers, B. P. M. (1994) *The Effective Classroom*. London: Cassell.

Fullan, M. (1991) *The New Meaning of Educational Change*. London: Cassell.

Fullan, M. (1995) 'The school as a learning organisation: distant dreams'. *Theory into Practice* **34**(4), Autumn, 230–35.

Good, T. L. and Brophy, J. E. (1980) *Looking in Classrooms*, 2nd edn. New York: Harper and Row.

Gray, J. and Wilcox, B. (1995) *Good School, Bad School: Evaluating Performance and Encouraging Improvement*. Milton Keynes: Open University Press.

Hargreaves, A. (1995) 'Renewal in the age of paradox', *Educational Leadership*, April, 14–19.

Harris, A. (1996) 'Effective teaching', in *School Improvement Network Bulletin*. London: Institute of Education.

Hook, C. (1963) *Education for Modern Man*. New York: Alfred Knoff.

Hopkins, D. (1993) *A Teacher's Guide to Classroom Research,* 2nd edn. Milton Keynes: Open University Press.

Hopkins, D. (1996) 'Towards a theory for school improvement', in Gray, J. *et al.*, *Merging Traditions*. London : Cassell.

Hopkins, D. (1997) 'Powerful learning, powerful teaching and powerful schools'. Occasional Paper Series, Centre for Teacher and School Development, University of Nottingham.

Hopkins, D., Ainscow, M., West, M. (1994) *School Improvement in an Era of Change*. London: Cassell.

Hopkins, D. and West, M. (1994) 'Teacher development and school improvement', in Walling, D (ed.), *Teachers as Leaders: Perspectives on the Professional Development of Teachers*. Bloomington, Indiana: Phi Delta Kappa.

Hopkins, D. and Terrell, I. (1995) *Summative Evaluation of TVEI in Essex*. Cambridge: University of Cambridge Institute of Education.

Hopkins, D., West, M., Ainscow, M. (1996) *Improving the Quality of Education for All*. London: David Fulton Publishers.

Hopkins, D., West, M., Beresford, J. (1998) 'Creating the conditions for classroom and teacher development'. *Teachers and Teaching: Theory and Practice* (in press).

Johnson, D. W. and Johnson, R. T. (1989) *Leading the Co-operative School*. Edina: Interaction Book Company.

Joyce, B. (1992) 'Cooperative learning and staff development: teaching the method with the method', *Cooperative Learning* **12** (2), 10–13.

Joyce, B., Showers, B., Rolheiser-Bennett, C. (1987) 'Staff development and student learning: a synthesis of research on models of teaching', *Educational Leadership* **45** (2), 11–23.

Joyce, B., Wolf, J. and Calhoun, E. (1993) *The Self Renewing School*. Alexandria VA ASCD.

Joyce, B. and Showers, B. (1995) *Student Achievement through Staff Development*, 2nd edn. New York: Longman.

Joyce, B. and Weil, M. (1996) *Models of Teaching*, 5th edn. Englewood Cliffs, New Jersey: Prentice-Hall.

Joyce, B., Calhoun, E., Hopkins, D. (1997) *Models of Learning – Tools for Teaching*. Milton Keynes: Open University Press.

Kolb, D. (1984) *Experiential Learning*. Englewood Cliffs, New Jersey: Prentice-Hall.

Marzano, R. J. *et al.* (1992) *Dimensions of Learning*. Teacher's Manual. Aurora: ASCD/McREL.

OFSTED (1994) *Improving Schools*. London: HMSO.

OFSTED (1995) *The Annual Report of Her Majesty's Chief Inspector of Schools. Part 1*. London: HMSO.

Peters, R. S. (1974) *Psychology and Ethical Development*. London: George Allen and Unwin.

Rogers, C. (1983) *Freedom to Learn*, 2nd edn. Columbus, Ohio: Merrill.

Sharnbrook Upper School (1995) *Sharnbrook Learning Project: Report of Phase One*. Bedford: Sharnbrook Upper School.

Slavin, R. E. (1993) 'Co-operative learning in OECD countries: research, practice and prevalence'. Centre for Educational Research and Innovation, Organization for Economic Co-operation and Development.

West, M. and Hopkins, D. (1996) 'Reconceptualising school effectiveness and school improvement'. Paper presented at the Annual Meeting of AERA, New York, April 1996.

Wheldall, K. and Merrett, M. (1989) *Positive Teaching in the Secondary School*. London: Paul Chapman.